Cognitive-Behavioral Treatment of Depression

CLINICAL APPLICATION OF EVIDENCE-BASED PSYCHOTHERAPY

A Series of Books Edited By
William C. Sanderson

In response to the demands of the new health care environment, there is a movement in psychology (and in all of health care) toward defining empirically supported treatment approaches (i.e., treatments that have been shown to be effective in controlled research studies). The future demands of psychotherapy are becoming clear. In response to pressures from managed care organizations and various practice guidelines, clinicians will be required to implement evidence-based, symptom-focused treatments.

Fortunately, such treatments exist for a variety of the most commonly encountered disorders. However, it has been extremely difficult to disseminate these treatments from clinical research centers, where the treatments are typically developed, to practitioners. More often than not, the level of detail in treatment protocols used in research studies is insufficient to teach a clinician to implement the treatment.

This series, *Clinical Application of Evidence-Based Psychotherapy*, will address this issue. For each disorder covered, empirically supported psychological procedures will be identified. Then, an intensive, step-by-step, session-by-session treatment application will be provided. A detailed clinical vignette will be woven throughout, including session transcripts.

All books in this series are written by experienced clinicians who have applied the treatments to a wide variety of patients, and have supervised and taught other clinicians how to apply them.

Cognitive-Behavioral Treatment of Depression

JANET S. KLOSKO, Ph.D.
and
WILLIAM C. SANDERSON, Ph.D.

JASON ARONSON INC.
Northvale, New Jersey
London

This book was set in 11 pt. New Aster by Alpha Graphics in Pittsfield, New Hampshire and printed and bound by Book-mart Press, Inc. of North Bergen, New Jersey.

Library of Congress Cataloging-in-Publication Data
Klosko, Janet S.
    Cognitive-behavioral treatment of depression / Janet S. Klosko and William C. Sanderson.
        p. cm.
    Includes index.
    ISBN 0-7657-0152-9 (alk. paper)
    1. Depression, Mental—Treatment. 2. Cognitive therapy. 3. Brief psychotherapy. I. Sanderson, William C. II. Title.
RC537.K565 1998
616.85'270651—dc21   97-43073

Printed in the United States of America on acid-free paper. Jason Aronson offers books and cassettes. For information and catalog write to Jason Aronson Inc., 230 Livingston Street, Northvale, New Jersey 07647-1726. Or visit our website: http://www.aronson.com

CONTENTS

III
Behavioral Treatments

**APPENDIX II: Supporting Studies:
Selected References of Controlled Studies**

ACKNOWLEDGMENTS

I would like to acknowledge the supervisors who have guided me through the years to become the clinician I am today: Jeffrey Young, David Barlow, Jayne Rygh, Will Swift, Ann De Lancey, Mike Burkhardt, Glen Conrad, Robert Boice, John Wapner, and Robin Tassinari. I would also like to acknowledge my colleagues: Bill Sanderson, Ken Appelbaum, Alan Cohen, and Bob Shugoll. There is a piece of each of you in this book.

—J. S. K.

First, I would like to acknowledge the individuals who have been directly involved and have had a significant influence on my professional development: David H. Barlow, Aaron T. Beck, Susan G. O'Leary, and Jeffrey Young. I would also like to acknowledge T. Byram Karasu, Chairman of the Psychiatry Department at Albert Einstein College of Medicine, who has provided me with the opportunity to be productive in my academic endeavors. Numerous colleagues have served as collaborators, advisers, and friends over the years, including Tim Bruce, Janet Klosko, Alec Miller, Lata McGinn, Ron Rapee, Jill Rethus, and Scott Wetzler. Finally, I would like to acknowledge the many patients I have treated who have provided the motivation and challenge to evolve as a psychotherapist.

—W. C. S.

I

GENERAL
PRINCIPLES

TREATMENT RATIONALE

The Cognitive-Behavioral Model of Depression

Within the cognitive-behavioral model, cognition, mood, physiology, and behavior are all important aspects of the experience of depression. They are different components of the same phenomenon. They interact, they can all be causal at different times, and all serve to maintain the person's depression.

A depressive episode is usually triggered by a negative event. It might be the loss of a love relationship, an experience of failure in one's work, the loss of a significant other's positive regard, or some other blow to the person's self-esteem. As B. F. Skinner put it, the person loses some source of positive reinforcement.

It is normal for a person to feel sadness following a loss. The experience of sadness moves the person toward acceptance of the loss and eventual emotional disengagement. However, in depression, the sense of loss becomes abnormally generalized—to the whole world and to the whole self. The person feels hopeless and helpless.

Once the process begins it becomes a downward spiral, with cognition, mood, physiology, and behavior all triggering one another, resulting in increasing depression. Negative thoughts, depressed mood, agitated or slowed physiology, and passive or withdrawn behavior all roll together into a snowball that propels the person downward. It becomes a vicious cycle: the person gets less positive reinforcement from life, and, feeling hopeless to improve things, the person does and gets increasingly less.

Case Example

Let us watch this process unfold in Luke, a patient we present to illustrate the cognitive-behavioral treatment of depression. Luke wants to be a police officer but fails the examination. He goes on a drinking binge, and, hungover, mishandles a job interview. "I felt like a real loser," he says. "I didn't think I'd ever succeed at anything." Luke withdraws into himself, stops calling his friends, stops going out, and stays home and broods. When his friends visit he is flat and uncommunicative. Gradually his friends visit less. Luke stops exercising, drinks too much, eats too little, and sleeps too much: "I felt, what was the point of doing anything? Nothing seemed to matter." He spends whole weekends in bed in his bathrobe. One evening, finding himself staring at the wall for hours thinking about the best way to commit suicide, he finally decides to seek help. "Thinking about suicide gave me a sense of comfort," he says.

In Luke we can see the way negativity breeds negativity in depression.

Cognitive-Behavioral Treatment

As cognitive-behavioral therapists, we try to intervene at all the levels of depression. We teach patients to manage their cognitions, mood, physiology, and behavior better so they can overcome their depression and meet their goals in life.

At the cognitive level, we teach patients cognitive therapy techniques so they can correct their negatively distorted depressive thoughts and think more realistically. At the level of mood, we teach them self-control techniques so they can better contain and manage their negative emotions. At the physiological level, we teach them to use imagery, meditation, and relaxation techniques to calm their bodies and center their attention. And we use behavioral techniques such as activity scheduling and assertiveness training to help them behave in more constructive ways.

In our use of these techniques, we try to create a positive spiral where, instead of getting less and less—the common scenario in depression—the person is able to utilize these strategies and get more and more from life. We try to support cognitions, moods, physiological states, and behaviors that trigger positive responses and help the person climb out of the depression.

We ally with the patient's healthy side. Cognitive-behavioral therapy is an approach that finds what is healthy and builds upon it. The basic model of treatment is one of empowering the patient. This is short-term therapy, and the emphasis is on giving patients the skills they need to overcome their depression as quickly as possible and to maintain their gains on their own.

QUALITIES OF THE
THERAPEUTIC RELATIONSHIP

General Considerations

No matter what school of therapy we identify as our own, to be effective as therapists we must demonstrate the classic non-specific characteristics identified as important by therapy process researchers: empathy, warmth, and genuineness.

One mistake we sometimes see in therapists starting out in cognitive-behavioral therapy is a tendency to spend too little time focused on building the relationship with patients. They are too mechanical, too emotionless. They view their function as imparting information and instructing patients, and regard building the relationship as a waste of time. But when too little time is given to building the relationship, patients find it difficult to improve. Research demonstrates that successful cognitive-behavioral therapy patients view the therapy relationship as crucial in helping them change.

Effective cognitive-behavioral therapists are warm rather than detached and aloof. They are human rather than godlike. They try not to appear as though they are perfect, or as though they have knowledge they are withholding from the patient. They strive to make the patient feel understood and accepted. They let their natural personality come through. They share their emotional responses when they know it will have a positive effect on the patient. They self-disclose when it will help the patient (when it concerns problems the therapist has worked out successfully). They strive for a compassionate, nonattached stance toward patients.

In aiming for this kind of open, collaborative relationship, cognitive-behavioral therapists are opposed to classical psychoanalytic therapists, who have traditionally aimed for neutrality. To maximize transference, classical psychoanalytic therapists have attempted to become "blank slates" onto which patients can project significant relationships from their past. Working through the transference is the center of the treatment. Cognitive-behavioral therapy has a whole different spirit. The therapist does not have the goal of maximizing transference. The therapist strives to be a real person who cares about the patient, who understands the patient, and whom the patient can trust. Solving problems in the patient's current life—rather than the therapy relationship—is the center of the treatment. This is not to say that the therapist ignores therapy process. The therapy relationship provides another set of opportunities to apply the principles of cognitive-behavioral therapy. (We recognize that some patients, for example, those with axis II diagnoses, particularly personality disorders, require more focus on the therapy relationship as part of their treatment, and may not be able to benefit significantly from short-term treatment.)

We use the model of "empathize, validate, confront." Here is an example from a session with Luke. The therapist was encouraging him to start going out with his friends again.

> *Luke:* I just have no desire to see people, to go out. I don't know what to say. People ask me how I am, and the truth is that I'm lousy. People ask me what's going on, and nothing's going on. It's depressing. I just feel more depressed when I go out. Why put myself through that?
>
> *Therapist:* I see what you mean. You don't see the point of going out when you feel like you'll just have a bad time anyway.

> *Luke:* I'll just end up drinking too much. That's what'll happen. I won't be able to handle it. At home I might be bored, but at least I'm comfortable. I don't have to deal with anything.
>
> *Therapist:* I can see how overwhelming the whole thing seems to you. (Pause.) What would have to happen for you to feel that it *had* worked to go out, that you *had* handled the situation?
>
> *Luke:* What would have to happen? I don't know. I guess I would have to talk to people, not be a downer for everyone involved, not get dead drunk. I would have to have a good time. Not get depressed.
>
> *Therapist:* What would you have to do to make that happen?
>
> *Luke:* Well, like I said, I'd have to talk to people. I'd have to ask them about themselves, and not be so self-absorbed. And I'd have to not drink. Drinking couldn't be involved at all, that's for sure.

Before moving into an intervention, the therapist let Luke express his feelings about the issue at hand, and the therapist empathized with and validated those feelings. Then Luke was more ready to contemplate ways of mastering the situation of going out with his friends.

In the model of "empathize, validate, confront," first we allow patients to tell their stories and to vent. We try to immerse ourselves in their phenomenological world so that we can empathize as fully as we can. We mirror back to them what they are saying and what they are feeling. We tell them that we understand, that their stories and their feelings make sense. Only then do we confront their sense of passivity and powerlessness. Until patients feel understood, it is difficult to make headway in challenging their cognitions.

Further, encouraging patients to vent their feelings during sessions increases their emotional involvement with the session material, which in turn promotes their progress in treatment. A core principle of cognitive-behavioral therapy is that change is most likely to take place when patients are processing experiences on an emotional level. Processing material in the presence of affect helps patients make the shift from purely intellectual understanding to emotional acceptance.

As much as possible, short-term cognitive-behavioral therapists keep treatment focused on the present. Their goal is to help patients solve the problems they are having *now*. Although they recognize that the past is important and they discuss it when necessary, they do not get lost in the past. If a discussion of the past will help patients solve their current problems, then the therapist keeps the discussion short and to the point. The therapist empathizes with the patient and validates the patient's feelings, but then moves the discussion back into the present. (There are exceptions to this. For example, the patient might have another disorder, such as posttraumatic stress disorder, in which case it is necessary for the therapist to focus upon the past in order to treat the other disorder. Alternatively, patients might have characterological problems that interfere with their progress in cognitive-behavioral treatment. Such patients usually require treatment that includes more of a focus on the past—particularly childhood—and identification of lifelong patterns.)

Collaborative Empiricism

Beck (1995) uses the term *collaborative empiricism* to characterize the nature of the therapist–patient relationship in cognitive therapy. The therapist is active and directive. Therapist and patient collaborate together on a rational approach to the patient's current life, using the principles of logic and the scientific method. Together they identify the patient's thoughts and underlying assumptions. They treat these thoughts and assumptions as hypotheses that can be tested.

To foster this spirit of collaborative empiricism, cognitive-behavioral therapists typically begin treatment by educating patients about their disorder. They recommend books and articles for patients to read (e.g., *Feeling Good* by David Burns). They teach patients about the signs and symptoms of their disorder. They inform patients about helpful research findings. When they present a new technique, they always begin by presenting the rationale. Educating patients in these ways helps build the therapeutic alliance.

Cognitive-behavioral therapists provide structure. Therapist and patient together agree upon the goals of therapy and make these goals explicit. A simple list that both can go back and review works well. The goals are specific and concrete (e.g., "decreasing depressive symptoms" rather than "feeling better"). The therapist and the patient continually evaluate how well therapy is helping the patient progress toward these goals, and the therapist modifies treatment strategies and goals when appropriate. Empathically but persistently, the therapist keeps returning to the goals the two have set.

The therapist starts each session by setting an agenda of topics to cover during that session. Usually the agenda begins with patients briefly describing their experience since the last session, including doing their homework assignments.

> *Therapist:* Let's make the agenda for this session. First, you can catch me up on your week and tell me about doing your homework. Do you have anything you want to put on the agenda?

Luke: I've been having trouble sleeping. I want to talk about that.

Therapist: Okay. (Writes.) Is there anything else?

Luke: Yeah, I ran into my old girlfriend, I wanted to talk about that. I filled out a thought record about it.

Therapist: Okay. (Writes.) Anything else?

Luke: No. That's pretty much it.

Therapist: I wanted to teach you some relaxation techniques, so I'll put that on the agenda, too.

It is up to the therapist to keep an overall sense of the time required to complete the agenda items and to time each one accordingly. The therapist and patient together come to some resolution or plan to deal with an item before going on to the next one. The therapist does not allow the patient to go from problem to problem without solving any of them.

What happens between sessions is important; the therapist puts great emphasis upon homework. By the end of each session, therapist and patient agree upon some "experiment" in the patient's current life designed to test beliefs and build skills. It is the therapist's responsibility to facilitate compliance with homework assignments. (One of the primary reasons patients are noncompliant with homework is that the therapist does not pay enough attention to it.) Providing a rationale that motivates patients, developing homework assignments in collaboration with the patient, following up with assignments, praising patients when they complete assignments, brainstorming solutions when problems occur, and pointing out the positive consequences of carrying out homework assignments are all ways the therapist can facilitate compliance.

Cognitive-behavioral therapists ask patients for feedback—about themselves, the treatment, each session. We encourage the patient to express negative feelings, or else they create distance and resistance. Our goal in responding to negative feedback is to listen without becoming defensive and to try to understand the situation from the patient's point of view. (Of course, we do not let the patient behave abusively—for example, speaking too loudly, making personal attacks—without setting limits.) If the patient's negative feedback is based on thoughts that are exaggerated or unrealistic, then we attempt to use it as an opportunity to help the patient identify and correct cognitive distortions. If the patient's negative feedback is accurate, then we acknowledge our part and attempt to use it as an opportunity to problem-solve together.

We believe therapists should aim to communicate a sense of calm faith in their ability to help the patient. This will ease the patient's feelings of hopelessness that are so much a part of the downward spiral of depression. An optimistic, persistent therapeutic style is especially useful in treating this patient population.

Guided Discovery

Beck (1995) uses the term *guided discovery* to describe what he believes is the best way to help patients identify particular cognitive errors. This is the Socratic method: rather than simply pointing out the errors (and perhaps seeming to lecture or reprimand patients), the therapist asks questions that direct patients to find the errors themselves. The rationale is that patients benefit more from discovering their own cognitive distortions; the process is more deeply convincing to them than simply being told what their distortions are. In addition, by asking directed questions, the therapist models a process patients can learn to use on their own. Merely pointing out patients' distortions is not likely to generalize to other situations.

However, teaching patients the process of evaluating their thoughts provides them with a tool they can use in many other situations.

The use of guided discovery points to a core principle of cognitive-behavior therapy: as much as possible, the therapist encourages patients to generate their own solutions to problems. The therapist strives for an optimum level of helping—not so much that patients work below their capacity, but not so little that patients fail to find solutions altogether. The questions the therapist asks guide the patient toward a healthy response. For example, here is an excerpt from one of Luke's sessions. This followed the homework described above, of going out with friends. Luke is evaluating his performance.

Therapist: Well, how did you do?

Luke: Lousy. I did lousy.

Therapist: What makes you say that?

Luke: Oh, I was really quiet all night. I felt like I had nothing to say to anyone. Not drinking didn't help. I fell into a funk and had nothing to say.

Therapist: So you didn't talk to anyone the whole night?

Luke: Pretty much. I talked to my sister for a while. That wasn't too bad. But I could tell she thought I was a downer.

Therapist: How could you tell that? Did she put you down in some way or try to get away from you?

Luke: No, no. She was right there. But I could see it in her eyes.

Therapist: What could you see?

Luke: I don't know. That she felt sorry for me. That she was trying to be there for me. That she cares, really. (Pause.)

Therapist: Who else did you talk to?

Luke: Well, I talked to my friend Al. That wasn't really too bad either. He was telling me that he went through problems, was seeing a therapist for a while. That surprised me. I never thought of Al as a guy who would ever see a therapist.

Therapist: Did anyone do anything that made you feel like they didn't want you there, that you were a "downer"?

Luke: Nah, I guess not. When we left everyone was really nice, telling me to call them and all.

Instead of telling Luke, "There you go again, minimizing the positive and jumping to conclusions," the therapist asked questions that encouraged Luke to examine the evidence himself. The therapist's questions guided the patient to revise the way he was thinking about the situation. Ideally, patients are able to internalize this process, and learn to evaluate the evidence for their feelings on an ongoing basis as they go through their lives.

OVERCOMING OBSTACLES TO TREATMENT

Some common problems are (1) noncompliance, (2) inability to grasp the cognitive model, and (3) persistence of depressive symptoms despite use of the model. We will discuss each of these problems in turn.

Noncompliance

Patients might demonstrate noncompliance with treatment procedures. For example, they might cancel sessions or come to sessions late, resist focusing on session material, or fail to carry out homework assignments.

To develop a strategy for addressing noncompliance, it is necessary to know why the patient is resisting. For example, a patient who is noncompliant with homework assignments because approaching the homework provokes intense anxiety requires a different strategy than a patient who is noncompliant because he or she did not understand the homework in the first place but was too unassertive to say so. Other possible causes of noncompliance are pessimism, fear of changing, secondary gain for maintenance of symptoms, interfering variables in the patient's environment, and problems in the therapist–patient relationship.

Thus, the first step in dealing with noncompliance is to assess the cause of the problem. Sometimes the therapist can accomplish this simply by asking the patient. The patient can say, "I don't understand the point of this technique," "Using this technique makes me anxious," "I felt too hopeless to do the homework," "The homework seemed too hard for me," "I forgot." When this happens, the therapist can work with the patient to develop a plan for dealing with the problem.

However, often patients cannot or will not tell the therapist why they are noncompliant. When this happens, the therapist can say to the patient, "The part of you that did not want to do the homework (or follow a session procedure, etc.), what was that part feeling? What was that part thinking?" Sometimes phrasing the question this way enables patients to answer. Then, the therapist can use the opportunity to empathize with the resistant part of the patient before moving into an intervention.

The therapist can also ask the patient, "The part of you that *did* want to do the homework, what was that part feeling and thinking?" This allows the patient to verbalize the positive consequences of following through on the homework. The therapist can ask the patient to express what both the healthy and the resistant sides felt, so that the patient feels fully heard. (The therapist can even have the two sides dialogue with one another in the session and negotiate a solution to the problem.)

As much as possible, the therapist guides patients to discover their own solutions for their noncompliance rather than suggesting solutions to them. The therapist encourages patients to take a problem-solving approach, using the techniques they are learning in treatment: What are the thoughts patients are having about the part of treatment they are resisting? Are those thoughts rational? What is the evidence that supports the thoughts? What is the evidence that refutes them? What steps can patients take to overcome their resistance to treatment?

Even if the therapist feels it, the therapist should not express annoyance when patients are noncompliant. Responding to patients' noncompliance with hostility is likely to have a destructive impact on the treatment. We suggest that you observe your own anger at the patient but that you do not act on it. Strive to maintain a compassionate, nonattached stance, and attempt to view noncompliant patients as doing the best they can. Take the view that everything that happens in therapy can be an opportunity to build the therapeutic alliance, and try to use the patient's noncompliance in some positive way— preferrably as a problem you two can solve together. Within even the most resistant patient is a healthy side that wants to change. Try to join with the patient's healthy side in fighting the side that resists. Empathize with how difficult it is for patients to change, while at the same time encouraging them to articulate the negative consequences of noncompliance.

Persistent noncompliance with treatment procedures, despite reasonable efforts to address the problem, is one predictor that the patient will have a negative response to short-term cognitive-behavioral therapy. Such noncompliance might be a sign of underlying characterological problems and is one indication that the patient requires longer-term treatment.

Inability to Grasp the Cognitive Model

Sometimes patients are not able to grasp the cognitive model. They are not able to distance themselves from their thoughts and feelings in order to explore their own role in constructing reality. In Piaget's (1967) terms, these patients have not reached the "formal operations" stage of cognitive development. When this happens, it is important for the therapist to adapt the model to fit the patient's level of cognitive development. The therapist can focus on the most concrete, behavioral aspects of the model and encourage the patient to work with these.

For example, rather than having the patient evaluate cognitions, the therapist can teach the patient to use coping self-statements in difficult situations. Coping self-statements are rational responses to the patient's negative thoughts and feelings and behavioral instructions. The therapist and patient compose the coping self-statements together, rather than relying on the patient to generate them alone. For example, a patient who feels self-conscious in social situations might utilize these coping self-statements: "I'm only imagining that everyone's focused on me. Other people are focused on themselves, not on me. These feelings of anxiety will pass and I will be comfortable again. Right now I can breathe slowly and deeply and center my body and mind. I can focus on enjoying being with and talking to other people. Right now I'm going to find one person I would like to talk to and start a conversation." You can write the coping self-statements on a flash card—an index card or other small piece of paper—that patients can carry with them and read whenever they feel the need.

Persistence of Depressive Symptoms Despite Use of the Model

As patients learn to use cognitive-behavioral techniques, it is common for them to say something like, "Even though I *know* that my thoughts are irrational, I still *feel* like they are true. I still *feel* the same." When this happens, encourage patients to keep practicing the techniques. Tell them that this is a common complaint, and that it usually yields to repeated practice. Research shows that thoughts, feelings, and behavior all change at different rates in therapy. Generally, behavior changes first, then thoughts, and then feelings change last. Repeated practice will help many of these patients make the shift from "knowing" to "feeling," and they will gradually come to accept the changes in their thinking on a deeper, more emotional level.

Some patients will not respond positively to cognitive-behavioral therapy, even with repeated practice. However, many patients will benefit significantly, and will be able to continue improving on their own. (We further discuss treatment nonresponders in Session 7 of our program.)

II

EIGHT
COGNITIVE-BEHAVIORAL
TREATMENT SESSIONS

AN OVERVIEW

In this section, we begin by describing the characteristics of patients who are appropriate candidates for short-term, cognitive-behavioral treatment. We then discuss the timing of sessions. Next, we list the standard cognitive-behavioral treatment components that occur in all the sessions. We then briefly describe the behavioral treatments. Finally, we provide an outline of the eight-session treatment.

Who Is an Appropriate Candidate for Short-Term, Cognitive-Behavioral Treatment?

Not every depressed patient is an appropriate candidate for short-term cognitive-behavioral treatment. Mild-to-moderately depressed patients are more likely to benefit than more severely depressed patients. Patients with severe depression (i.e., a score of 20 or higher on the Beck Depression Inventory [see Appendix I]) will probably require longer-term treatment. Further, patients who have additional axis I or axis II disorders are less likely to benefit than patients who do not have additional disorders. Patients with psychotic features, bipolar disorder, current substance abuse, or severe personality disorder diagnoses (such as borderline personality disorder) are not appropriate candidates for this treatment and should be screened out.

Research shows that the ideal patients for short-term, cognitive-behavioral treatment—those who are most likely to have a positive response—tend to have the following characteristics: they are above average in intelligence, they are able to access their thoughts and feelings, they are capable of forming meaningful interpersonal relationships, they are highly motivated, they are able to accept personal responsibility for changing in therapy, and they are optimistic about their potential for change.

The Timing of Sessions

The sessions do not necessarily have to occur once a week. We recommend that you adjust the schedule to fit the needs of each patient. We have found, however, that a schedule that tends to work well for mild-to-moderately depressed patients is conducting the earlier sessions once a week, then spacing out the later sessions to every other week or even once per month. That way, patients can wean themselves from therapy gradually, rather than stopping abruptly.

Severely depressed patients will probably require more frequent sessions, especially at the beginning of therapy, and some may require sessions twice a week.

Standard Cognitive-Behavioral Treatment Components

Each session contains the following standard cognitive-behavioral treatment components:

1. Setting the agenda for the session
2. Reviewing homework assignments completed since the last session
3. Assigning new homework
4. Asking for feedback about the session

Behavioral Treatments

Starting in the fourth session, the therapist introduces behavioral treatments for problems that frequently co-occur with depression, such as interpersonal problems, anger-control problems, stress-management problems, low productivity, and excessive anxiety. The therapist selects the behavioral treatments that are most applicable to each patient. The behavioral treatments are in Part III of this book, and include the following:

1. Assertiveness training
2. Anger management
3. Relaxation techniques
4. Improving productivity
5. Managing panic attacks
6. Managing worry.

Outline of Treatment

We present the treatment as follows:

Session 1
1. Education about depression
2. Suicide assessment and contract
3. Scheduling pleasurable activities
4. Establishing a basic structure for each day

Session 2
1. The cognitive model of depression
2. Self-monitoring of automatic thoughts

Session 3
1. Examining the evidence
2. Generating alternatives

Session 4
  1. Cognitive distortions
  2. Introduction of appropriate behavioral treatment

Session 5
  1. Hypothesis testing
  2. Problem solving
  3. Continuing appropriate behavioral treatment

Session 6
  1. Identifying and evaluating underlying assumptions and
     schemas
  2. Continuing appropriate behavioral treatment

Session 7
  1. Summary of the steps of cognitive therapy
  2. Relapse prevention (for treatment responders)
  3. Continuing appropriate behavioral treatment

Session 8 (for treatment responders)
  1. Plan for maintenance and generalization
  2. Termination

SESSION 1

- Set the agenda
  - Education about depression
  - Suicide assessment and contract
  - Scheduling pleasurable activities
  - Establishing a basic structure for each day
- Assign homework
- Ask for feedback about the session

Set the Agenda

Briefly list the topics you wish to cover this session and ask patients if they have topics they wish to cover. Write down the agenda items as you and the patient agree upon them so you can refer to the list in the course of the session.

Education about Depression

Give patients their Mastering Depression Notebook. This is any plain loose-leaf notebook where patients can keep all their handouts, self-monitoring forms, session notes, and homework assignments. Patients will have this notebook to refer to after treatment ends.

Have the patient complete the Beck Depression Inventory (see Appendix I). Discuss the results with the patient. You can use this scale to interpret the patient's score:

Total Score	Level of Depression
0–9	Mild
10–19	Moderate
20–29	Severe
30–39	Very severe
≥ 40	Profound

In addition, discuss individual items with the patient, especially ones on which the patient scored high. Pay particular attention to item 2, concerning hopelessness, and item 9, concerning suicidal ideation.

Place the scored form in the patient's file. That way you will have a pretreatment measure of the patient's depression, allowing you to evaluate the effectiveness of your intervention more objectively.

Present the following information to patients. In addition, give them the "Education about Depression" handout (see Appendix I) to put in their notebook.

The Symptoms of Depression

Therapist: According to the 1994 *Diagnostic and Statistical Manual of Mental Disorders* (*DSM-IV*) (American Psychiatric Association 1994), the book professionals use to diagnose emotional problems, the symptoms of depression are as follows. If you are depressed, you probably have most (but not necessarily all) of these symptoms.

1. Depressed mood: This means that most of the time you feel down, sad, empty, discouraged. You may cry a lot, or you may be unable to cry. Feeling irritable is another common emotional symptom, especially in children and adolescents who are depressed.

2. Loss of interest: You have a loss of interest and pleasure in life so that you have to push yourself to do things you used to enjoy. This often includes a loss of interest in sex. It becomes difficult for you to anticipate that any activity might be pleasurable.

3. Change in appetite for food: The most usual picture is that you lose your appetite. Food neither interests

you nor appeals to you. You have to push yourself to eat, and may lose weight. Sometimes people eat more when they are depressed. They use food as a source of comfort or as a way to fill a sense of emptiness. If this is true of you, you may gain rather than lose weight.

4. Disturbed sleep: You sleep much less or much more than normal. If you are sleeping too little, you may have trouble falling asleep, you may keep waking during the night, or you may wake up too early and be unable to go back to sleep. If you are sleeping too much, you may be napping for long periods during the day, or you may be sleeping longer during the night.

5. Psychomotor agitation or retardation: Your body, your mind, and your speech are either going too fast or going too slow. Either you are agitated and restless, or you are sluggish.

6. Loss of energy: You feel tired, drained, fatigued. Even small tasks seem exhausting. In extreme cases, you find it hard to perform the normal activities of everyday life, such as showering, dressing, shopping, preparing food, and so on.

7. Feelings of worthlessness or guilt: You have low self-esteem. You brood about how worthless or bad you are. Possibly you hate yourself. You may feel that your depression is a punishment that you deserve. In addition, you are probably angry at yourself about how much you let depression impair your functioning.

8. Difficulty thinking: Your ability to think—to concentrate, make decisions—is impaired.

9. Suicidal ideation. You feel hopeless. You may have recurrent thoughts that life is not worth living or you would rather be dead. You may believe that others would be better off without you. You may fantasize about committing suicide, and may actually develop a plan for where, when, and how you are going to do it.

It is important that you share with me all your thoughts about suicide. If at any point during treatment you feel that you might attempt suicide or any form of self-harm, contact me (or the doctor-on-call if you are unable to get in touch with me) immediately. We'll talk about this more later in the session.

Depression may occur in one or more intense episodes (major depressive disorder), or it may underlie your life at a less intense level most of the time for years (dysthymic disorder).

Depressive episodes occur twice as frequently among women as among men (but equally as often for girls and boys). Both major depression and dysthymia tend to run in families. Rates of depression are not related to ethnicity, education, income, or marital status.

Depression can begin at any age (the average age of onset is the mid-20s). An untreated depressive episode usually lasts six months or longer. Following first episodes of depression, many people return to normal and never experience depression again. However, a significant portion of people who experience a first episode do not return to normal afterward. Rather, their depression becomes chronic, and they become dysthymic or they have recurrent episodes (or both).

Depression May Have a Physical Cause

Therapist: Before pursuing therapy for your depression, you should rule out possible physical causes. Depression may be due to the direct physical effects of a substance you are abusing (e.g., alcohol, cocaine), or of a prescribed medication (e.g., steroids, tranquilizers). Some medical treatments can trigger depression, as can some general medical conditions (e.g., hypothyroidism, stroke), and some toxins in the environment.

When there is a direct physical cause for your depression, there may be a direct physical cure—stopping the drug abuse, consulting your doctor about possible changes in your medication, correcting the medical condition, removing the toxin. All these avenues should be explored carefully before relying on therapy.

If you have not already had one, we recommend a thorough physical examination before beginning therapy for depression. We also recommend that you inform your physician about your participation in therapy.

Associated Features of Depression

Therapist: There are a number of signs that tend to be associated with depression. You may display any number of them: irritability, brooding, anxiety (e.g., obsessions, panic attacks, phobias, general anxiety), somatic complaints (e.g., headaches, gastrointestinal disturbance, muscle or joint pain). Women often experience a worsening of symptoms on the days before menstruation.

Be sure to inform me about any associated features of your depression.

Other Mental Disorders that Co-Occur with Depression

Therapist: Other mental disorders that frequently co-occur with depression include substance abuse, anxiety disorders (including posttraumatic stress), eating disorders, personality disorders, and attention-deficit disorders. In addition, some depressed individuals also go through episodes of mania. If you think you have symptoms of any of these other disorders, be sure to inform me so that your treatment can address these symptoms as well.

Cognitive-Behavioral Treatment of Depression

Therapist: Research has shown that cognitive-behavioral therapy is as good or better than other treatments, including antidepressant medication. Cognitive-behavioral therapy is particularly effective in the long run because it provides you with tools that you carry forward from treatment and continue to use. With medication alone, there is a higher risk of relapsing once the medication is discontinued.

Suggested Readings

Beck, A. T. (1976). *Cognitive Therapy and the Emotional Disorders*. New York: International Universities Press. (Softcover: New American Library, Dutton.)

Burns, D. D. (1980). *Feeling Good*. New York: William Morrow. (Softcover: New American Library, Penguin.)

Young, J. E., and Klosko, J. S. (1993). *Reinventing Your Life.* New York: New American Library, Dutton.

Suicide Assessment and Contract

Since depressed patients are at an increased risk for suicide, suicidal ideation must be assessed and monitored carefully throughout treatment. Suicide risk is especially high for individuals with psychotic features, a history of previous suicide attempts, a family history of completed suicides, or concurrent substance abuse. All of these factors should be assessed in the first session.

In addition to assessing psychotic features and substance abuse in the first session, ask the patient the following five questions. They assess current suicidal ideation, development of a plan, means and opportunity to carry out that plan, history of previous attempts, and suicidal intent. With each positive response the patient gives, suicide risk increases.

1. "Have you been feeling that you would rather be dead, or having thoughts of harming yourself in any way?"

    If the patient answers yes to this question, explore the frequency and intensity of the suicidal thoughts. Has the patient been having the thoughts often? How strong is the patient's desire to die? Why does the patient want to die? Is it to punish others? Is it a form of self-punishment? Is it to escape from pain? Does the patient have any reasons to live? Utter hopelessness is an important sign that the person is at risk.

2. "Have you been thinking about how you might harm yourself?"

    To assess active suicidal ideation, ask patients whether they have developed a specific plan for committing suicide. This might include jumping from a high place, overdosing on drugs or medication, using a gun or other weapon, getting into a car accident, or leaping in front of a train or bus. Do not suggest these plans to patients; rather, encourage them to describe fully what they have been imagining.

Suicide plans sometimes include specific times. Ask patients if they have thought about when they might like to die. Patients may plan to commit suicide on a certain date, such as a birthday, an anniversary of a special event, or a holiday. Plans sometimes include specific locations as well.

Patients may be having thoughts about passively harming themselves. For example, they might be planning to neglect their health by eating too little or too much, using alcohol or other drugs, or improperly taking prescription medicine. They might be planning to behave unsafely by carelessly crossing the street, driving recklessly, having promiscuous unprotected sex, or wandering alone at night in dangerous neighborhoods. They may display an attitude of willingness to take risks without caring what happens to them. If the patient answers yes to question 2, inquire about passive as well as active suicidal ideation.

3. "Do you think you would be able to carry out your plan?"

Once you understand the patient's plan, assess means and opportunity. Does the patient currently have access to a lethal dose of drugs, for example, or to a weapon? Is the patient likely to have such access in the future? When? Is the patient actively working on the plan already (e.g., collecting pills, applying for a gun license)? Will the patient have an opportunity soon to carry out the plan? Does the patient seem to have the will to carry out an attempt?

Can the patient name any deterrents? Is there anything that might keep the patient from making an actual attempt, such as religious convictions or concerns about hurting loved ones? Complete absence of deterrents is a strong danger sign.

4. "Have you ever tried to harm yourself in any way? To your knowledge, has anyone who is related to you by blood ever attempted to harm him- or herself?"

   If the patient has attempted suicide in the past, thoroughly assess all previous suicidal attempts and gestures. Remember to assess passive as well as active attempts. Has the patient ever been hospitalized? In addition, assess whether there is a family history of completed suicide.

5. "Do you think there is any chance whatsoever that you might attempt to hurt yourself, now or in the future?"

   Here you must gauge your own feelings as well as those expressed by your patient. If you feel uncomfortable or scared about letting the patient leave the session, then pay attention to your feelings.

   Ask the patient to estimate the odds of an actual attempt. Are they 50 percent? Lower? Higher? In the past few days, has the patient been feeling as though he or she might actually attempt suicide? Is the patient feeling this way now? Do these feelings distress the patient? Is the patient worried about losing control and attempting self-harm? Does the patient want help in preventing an attempt?

Has the patient been talking, reading, or writing about death or suicide recently? Has the patient been composing a suicide note, either in imagination or fact? What does the note say?

Explore whether the patient has made arrangements or set things in order in anticipation of an attempt. For example, the patient may have written a will, seen to the care of loved ones, given away personal belongings, or updated an insurance policy.

If the Patient Is Not Currently Suicidal: Making a Contract about Suicide

If your assessment convinces you that your patient is not currently suicidal, then ask him or her to agree to the following contract: So long as the patient is in treatment with you, the patient makes a commitment to discuss it with you (or the doctor-on-call if the patient is unable to get in touch with you) before attempting suicide or any form of self-harm. This contract includes passive as well as active suicidal ideation. The therapist must provide the patient with 24-hour access to an emergency service—usually a telephone answering service with a way to contact you (or the doctor-on-call) in case of an emergency.

Present this contract as a requirement of treatment. As an example, here is the way Luke's therapist presented it to him:

Therapist: I want to ask you something I ask every patient: I want to ask you to make a commitment that, if you ever feel like you're going to harm yourself in any way, you'll call me immediately and arrange to discuss it with me before you do anything to hurt yourself. If you can't reach me, you can contact the doctor-on-call, who will take care of you until I am able to connect with you.

Luke: What if I won't commit to that?
Therapist: Then I won't be able to treat you. I can't treat
    you unless I can be sure that you're safe.
Luke: I can make that commitment.

If the Patient Presents a Long-Term Suicide Risk but Is Not Imminently Suicidal

If the patient is not imminently suicidal but presents some long-term risk, the patient must agree to the following two conditions:

1. The patient must agree to be hospitalized if at any time during treatment the therapist (or the doctor-on-call) insists hospitalization is necessary to keep the patient safe.
2. The patient must agree to consult with a psychiatrist for evaluation and must follow through with the psychiatrist's recommendations, including accepting medication or hospitalization if necessary. The psychiatrist must have a 24-hour emergency line and admitting privileges.

Work with the patient to develop a plan for managing suicidal urges that allows both of you to feel secure and comfortable. Before the patient leaves the session, you should feel confident that the patient will not attempt suicide before the next session. The plan should contain a series of steps for the patient to follow when experiencing suicidal urges. The patient makes a commitment to follow the series of steps over and over until the urge passes or the patient is able to discuss it with you. You can then assess further the degree of imminent risk, and hospitalize the patient if necessary.

Some features the plan might include are filling out thought records about the urges, doing a self-control procedure such as meditation or relaxation, reading a list (constructed with the therapist) of reasons not to commit suicide, doing a problem-solving exercise, calling a friend, going outside for a walk, or going to a public place such as a restaurant or library. In severe cases, the plan can include such features as getting rid of any potentially lethal items (such as pills, weapons, or rope), not staying alone, calling a suicide hot line, or going to a hospital emergency room.

Additionally, the plan should involve the patient's agreement to refrain from taking drugs or alcohol until the urge has passed. If the patient is a substance-abuser, treatment should require that the patient do what is necessary to stop the substance abuse.

If the Patient Is Imminently Suicidal

If your assessment convinces you that the patient is imminently suicidal, then it is your responsibility to do everything possible to keep the patient safe (including breaking confidentiality, if necessary). The immediate goal is hospitalization. Do not leave the patient alone at any time until this has been accomplished. (If you are on the phone with the patient, stay on the phone until help arrives, or find someone else who can stay on the phone with the patient.) This means either taking the patient to the hospital yourself or making arrangements for someone else to do it.

If the patient refuses to go to the hospital, you have two choices. You can either call the police to take the patient to the hospital by force, or you can arrange for a significant other (relative, close friend) to stay with the patient. This person must understand the seriousness of the situation and commit to being with the patient at all times until the patient is out of the suicidal crisis. In addition to relying on this significant other, you should check in on the patient periodically—at least twice per day—until the crisis has passed. Make sure you have the patient's address and phone number, in case the patient calls you in a suicidal crisis and you have to send the police.

Dealing with suicidal patients is stressful. Remember to consult with your peers and your supervisors whenever a crisis arises.

Scheduling Pleasurable Activities

As always, begin by presenting the rationale.

> *Therapist:* Our immediate goal is to get you feeling better. Until you're feeling better it doesn't make sense to look at your life and the issues that are making you depressed. Your depression makes you too hopeless and negative about these things to be able to look at them objectively.
>
> In addition, withdrawing from activities you used to enjoy leads to decreased positive reinforcement in your life, thus increasing your depression. Getting you doing some of these activities again will break the cycle.
>
> The place to start is with what feels good. Is there anything you're enjoying? Are there any activities that you do that you still enjoy, even though you are depressed?
>
> *Luke:* No, not really. I don't enjoy anything. (Pause.) Well, that's not true. I do enjoy seeing my two nephews, my sister's kids. My sister's divorced, and I'm kind of like a father figure to her kids. Maybe seeing them,

and my sister, visiting them, playing ball with the kids. I still kind of enjoy that. At least I think I would. I haven't been over there in a long time.

Therapist: Let me write that down. (Writes.) You enjoy visiting your sister and her kids. That's very good. Is there anything else you still enjoy?

Luke: No, really, no.

Therapist: Then tell me some activities that you used to enjoy, before you were depressed. The last time you remember feeling happy, what were you doing?

Luke: Hmm, that's a hard one. The last time I can remember feeling happy was . . . maybe, months ago, last summer. I took my nephews camping. I like doing things like that with them. Physical, outdoor things, you know, like hiking, riding bikes, swimming.

Therapist: So you have enjoyed outdoor activities with your nephews. (Writes.) Very good. What else?

Luke: (Pause.) I can't think of anything.

Therapist: What are some of the things you've enjoyed doing in the past?

Luke: Well, I used to enjoy going out, you know, hanging out with friends.

Therapist: Doing what kind of things?

Luke: Well, I used to play volleyball every Thursday, and then go out afterward. I always liked that, but I stopped going months ago. I liked going out to dinner, going to movies, you know, the usual things. Going out on dates—now *that's* something I haven't done in a long time.

Go on this way until you have a list of activities the patient finds (or once found) pleasurable. Give the patient the handout Suggested Pleasurable Activities (see Appendix I). The patient can refer to it for ideas about pleasurable activities.

Once you have your list, ask the patient to agree to do at least one pleasurable activity each day. Patients can self-monitor on the Pleasurable Activities Self-Monitoring Form (see Appendix I). Here they record the date, time, and a brief description of the activity, and they record and rate their feelings before and after doing the activity. Almost always, patients find their mood improves, and doing the ratings lifts their morale.

It is customary for patients to do mastery and pleasure ratings as well. On the bottom of the form, patients can rate how much pleasure and how much of a sense of mastery they experienced while doing the activity. Patients should place all completed forms in their Mastering Depression Notebook.

Since they are not easily able to anticipate success, depressed patients are often skeptical about or resistant to doing these exercises. We have found that it is best not to get into a battle with patients to convince them that an exercise will work. Instead, we treat it as an experiment: we ask patients to agree to do the exercise, rating how they feel before and after, and then to come back to the next session and discuss their findings. This approach allows us to deal more effectively with their negativity and pessimism.

Establishing a Basic Structure for Each Day

If the patient's functioning is severely impaired so that he or she is spending a lot of time in bed, for example, then scheduling of pleasurable activities is not enough. If there are long periods of the day that the patient is doing nothing, then it is necessary to establish a basic structure for each day.

Make a contract that each day the patient will perform some basic activities of everyday life—getting showered and dressed, eating three healthy meals, physical exercise, work, socializing with others. You and the patient can make the list together, tailoring it to the specific patient's life. (Luke's list included studying for the police examination and attending Alcoholics Anonymous meetings.) Ask the patient to commit to doing every activity on the list every day.

Patients can record and rate their feelings before and after these activities as well. Again, they will almost always find that their mood improves as a result of doing the activities.

Assign Homework

Whenever you give a homework assignment, write it down in your notes using carbon paper so that you have two copies. Keep one copy, and give patients the other copy to put in their Mastering Depression Notebook.

The first homework assignment is for patients to do the activities in accord with the schedules you have discussed, filling out the appropriate self-monitoring forms.

In addition, ask patients to review the Education about Depression handout (see Appendix I) at least twice in the coming week, writing down any questions they may have in their notebook.

Remind patients to bring the notebook to the next session (and to every session), so that you can review the past week's work together and add new material.

Ask for Feedback about the Session

Ask patients if they have anything they would like to say about the session. Encourage them to express all their feelings. Mirror back what they are saying and how they are feeling. Aim to convey a sense of understanding and acceptance.

If it seems applicable, try to show patients how their feelings about the session are connected to their thoughts about it.

SESSION 2

- Set the agenda
- Review homework
  - The cognitive model of depression
  - Self-monitoring of automatic thoughts
- Assign homework
- Ask for feedback about the session

Set the Agenda

List briefly the topics you wish to cover and ask patients if they have any topics they wish to cover. Write down the list of agenda items.

Review Homework

Discuss the homework assignment. Openly express how pleased you are if the patient has done the homework. Review the homework with the patient thoroughly, emphasizing the positive consequences.

If the patient has not done the homework, explore the reasons. As we have noted, in order to come up with a successful strategy for addressing a patient's noncompliance with homework assignments, it is essential that you understand why the patient is not doing the homework. You can ask the patient, "The part of you that did not want to do the homework, what was that part feeling? What was that part thinking?" Attempt to identify cognitions related to not doing the assignment (e.g., pessimism, hopelessness). Then ask, "The part of you that *did* want to do the homework, what was that part feeling and thinking?" Your goal is to get the patient to verbalize the consequences of not doing the homework—that the patient is more likely to stay depressed—while at the same time validating the difficulties of doing the homework.

With very resistant patients, it sometimes helps to start with minimal homework requirements. Each week you can make slight increments.

The Cognitive Model of Depression

Introduce the Cognitive Model of Depression

The central idea of the cognitive model is that thoughts affect feelings. How we think about things affects how we feel about them.

Depressed people tend to think about reality in negatively distorted ways. Beck noticed that depressed patients tend to make certain characteristic cognitive distortions. Specifically, they make logical errors, such as jumping to conclusions or all-or-nothing thinking, and they fail to evaluate evidence objectively. They see the world through dark-colored glasses, thus increasing the likelihood that they will remain depressed.

Distorted negative thinking is a core feature of depression. Beck (Beck et al. 1979) discussed the "cognitive triad of depression," in which depressed patients have a negative view of the self, the world, and the future. The self is worthless, the world is overwhelming, and the future is hopeless. The cognitive triad serves as schemas for processing information. Since reality is filtered through these schemas, depressed patients consistently distort their interpretations of events to maintain the negative view of self, world, and future.

One major goal of cognitive-behavioral therapy is changing the distorted negative thinking. We do this in a number of ways: the primary methods are logical analysis, examining the evidence, and behavioral experiments. The goal is not *positive thinking*—for the patient to see the world through rose-colored glasses—but *realistic thinking*. The goal is for the patient to see the world more accurately, without the distorted dark lenses of depressive thought.

Introduce "Automatic Thoughts"

Intervening between events and the way we feel about them are our "automatic thoughts."

> *Therapist:* Our automatic thoughts are the thoughts and images that flow through our mind in response to an event. We say they are automatic because they are so familiar and habitual that we don't think about them. Often we're not even aware we're thinking them. We just accept them automatically. They are the givens in the way we think about our lives.
>
> Our automatic thoughts about events are an important determinant of how we respond emotionally to them.

Reliving an experience through imagery or role playing can help patients grasp the nature of automatic thoughts.

> *Therapist:* Let's do an imagery exercise to help you understand your automatic thoughts. Let's take something that you've brought up this session, something that happened this past week, and do an imagery exercise about it, something you felt strongly about.
>
> *Luke:* How about the dinner I had with Marybeth that got me so upset?
>
> *Therapist:* Okay, that's very good. Close your eyes and get an image of you and Marybeth at that dinner. Let an image come into your mind, and tell me what you see.

Luke: (Closes eyes.) I see the two of us there in the restaurant, and we're sitting there, and I'm trying to talk,
trying to make conversation, but her eyes are wandering, she's not looking at me. I start to feel really
crappy.

Therapist: What's going through your mind? What are you
thinking?

Luke: I'm thinking, "I'm a loser." I'm thinking, "I'm bor-
ing, I'm a loser, I can't keep the conversation
going."

Therapist: Those thoughts, those are your automatic
thoughts.

Times during sessions when patients display affect (e.g.,
crying, irritability) are useful as opportunities to elicit automatic thoughts. When you notice an intensification of affect,
help patients identify the thoughts and images that are going
through their minds. The presence of emotion makes it easier
for patients to identify their automatic thoughts, since the
thoughts are likely to be prominent.

Self-Monitoring of Automatic Thoughts

Give the patient self-monitoring forms (the Thought Record,
see Appendix I), and explain how to fill one out.

Therapist: I am going to give you these self-monitoring
forms. I want you to fill one out every time you have
a negative feeling. That is the cue to start filling out
a form—that you are having a negative feeling, a feeling like sadness, anxiety, guilt, anger.

Luke: If I have to fill one out every time I have a negative
feeling, then I'll be filling them out all day.

Therapist: If that's the case, you can set a criterion for filling them out. For example, you could say that you'll
fill one out every time you have an at least moderately strong negative feeling, like 50 or greater on a 0
to 100 scale. Or, to start, you could fill out two a day.
Would that make sense to you?

Luke: I could do that. I could do two a day.

Instruct patients to fill out a form as soon as possible upon
noticing the negative feeling. Research shows that the more
time passes, the more people forget their thoughts. The best
plan is to fill out the record as soon as the feeling begins, but
this is not always possible. Usually a patient cannot begin filling out forms while eating at a restaurant with a date, for example, or attending a meeting at work. In such cases patients
can only do their best and fill out the record as soon as possible afterward. While monitoring thoughts as soon as possible
is best, recalling them later is preferable to not monitoring
them at all.

Explain how to fill out each section of the self-monitoring
form. Use an example from the patient's life to illustrate. If possible, pick something the patient has brought up already that
session. It is important that the example you use be specific.

Therapist: Let's look at how to fill out the Thought Record.
The first part is the Upsetting Situation. This is whatever triggered your feeling. The upsetting situation
can be an event, like failing your practice test before
you came here today, but it can be a memory, it can
be a thought, or it can be an anticipation of a future
event. It can be a daydream. It's whatever you think
triggered your negative feeling.

Let's take an example. You came in today feeling depressed. What was the trigger? Was it failing your practice test before you came in, as you brought up?

Luke: Definitely. That's what got me going today. Failing that practice test.

Therapist: So that is what you would write there, for the Upsetting Situation.

Luke: (Writes.) For Situation, "failing my practice test."

Therapist: Okay, good. Now let's look at the next section. That's your feelings. What are the feelings you have about failing the practice test today?

Luke: Well, my feelings are anger at myself, that's the strongest feeling, and anxiety. It makes me really anxious when I fail these practice tests.

Therapist: So write "anger at myself" and "anxiety" there. Are there any other feelings?

Luke: No.

Therapist: Now, rate the strength of each feeling, from 0 to 100, with 25 being mild, 50 being moderate, 75 being severe, and 100 being as much as you can imagine. How strong is each feeling?

Luke: The anger at myself is strong, maybe 85, and the anxiety is a little less but it's still strong, maybe 70.

Therapist: Okay, good, so write those numbers next to the feelings.

Next, teach the patient how to fill out the Automatic Thoughts column.

Therapist: For the Automatic Thoughts column, I want you to write down the thoughts and images you're having about the upsetting event.

To do this, let part of yourself become an observer of your thoughts and images, just watching them and writing them down. Don't change the thoughts and images in any way; just write them down as they go through your mind.

Your automatic thoughts could include memories and fantasies as well. Maybe you're remembering the moment you found out you failed the last test, or maybe you're having a fantasy of failing the next one. Whatever it is that's going through your head, just write it down.

Let's go back to today, when you failed the practice exam. What were you thinking? What was going through your mind?

Luke: I was thinking that my brain is defective. That I'm stupid, you know?

Therapist: I see. Well, that's what you would write in the automatic thoughts column.

The patient can also rate how much he or she believes the automatic thought, on a 0 to 100 scale.

For the first week of recording, you can tell patients to leave the Rational Response and Re-Rate Emotions columns blank. This is because we want patients to focus on identifying their automatic thoughts rather than on challenging the thoughts.

Assign Homework

The homework for the second session is filling out a Thought Record whenever the patient experiences a negative feeling. Tell the patient to place all completed forms in the Mastering Depression Notebook, and to bring the notebook to the next session.

In addition, the patient should continue carrying out all agreed-upon activity schedules and recording them in the Mastering Depression Notebook.

Ask for Feedback about the Session

Ask patients if they have anything they would like to say about the session. Empathize with whatever patients say and validate their feelings. If patients express negative affect about the session, help them identify their automatic thoughts. Do not challenge the thoughts; just help patients to become aware of them and to tie them to their emotions.

SESSION 3

- Set the agenda
- Review homework
  - Examining the evidence
  - Generating alternatives
- Assign homework
- Ask for feedback about the session

Set the Agenda

State your agenda items for this session and ask patients if they have any items they would like to add. Write down the agenda items.

Review Homework

Review completed Thought Record forms that the patient has brought to the session. What did the patient learn? Discuss any problems the patient had in filling out the forms. As stated above, treat any noncompliance as a problem to be addressed in treatment. Identify any automatic thoughts that are responsible for noncompliance by completing a Thought Record with the patient.

Examining the Evidence

Examining evidence lies at the heart of a rational approach to life. When the patient's thoughts are about an empirical question, then the patient can test the accuracy of these thoughts by examining the evidence. This approach is more objective than basing thoughts on personal feelings or expectations.

Therapist: We're going to look now at filling out the Rational Response section of your thought monitoring form.

The first technique we're going to teach you is examining the evidence. The idea here is that, rather than just believing your automatic thoughts and assuming they are accurate, you are going to look at them objectively and test them where they can be tested by examining the evidence.

Let's look at an example. Let's look at your monitoring forms from this past week. Here's one. The trigger was "trying to study for the police exam." Your feelings were "anxiety: 70" and "self-hate: 85." Will you read your thoughts out loud? (Hands record to patient.)

Luke: My thoughts were, "I'm a loser. I'll never pass this exam."

Therapist: We'll let the fact that you called yourself a loser go for now, although that's an issue. But for now I want to focus on the prediction you just made, that you won't ever pass the exam. I want you to examine the evidence that you will never pass the test. Give me the evidence.

Luke: Well, I *feel* like I'll never pass.

Therapist: Yes, I know you do. But I want you to present the evidence like a trial lawyer, as though there were a jury sitting here and you had to argue each side. Only present evidence, like you do in court. Your feelings are not evidence you would present in court. You wouldn't get up in court and say, "I feel like it's true." What evidence would you present in court that you could never pass the test?

Luke: Okay, well, one piece of evidence I would present is that I failed the test once before. That seems like pretty strong evidence.

Therapist: Right, that is evidence. (Writes.) What else? What other evidence do you have that you'll fail the test?

Luke: Well, I've failed at other things. I didn't get into the college I wanted to go to. That's always bothered me. I ended up going to a college that wasn't as good. And since I left school I haven't done so great, going from job to job while I'm trying to make it into the police academy.

Therapist: Okay. (Writes.) Is there any other evidence?

Luke: Yeah, my brother always did better than me. He was better at just about everything—sports, school, friends, even women. In our family, he's the winner, and I'm the loser.

Therapist: Okay. (Writes.) Anything else?

Luke: (Thinks.) No, I can't think of anything else right now. Isn't that enough?

Therapist: Okay, so for supporting the idea that you won't be able to pass the police exam, the evidence you gave is the fact that you failed the exam once before, you didn't get into your top choice of colleges, you've moved from job to job since leaving college, and your brother did better than you at school, sports, friends, and women.

Let's do the other side. What is the evidence *against* the idea that you're going to fail the test? What's the evidence that this time you might pass?

Luke: Now that's a hard one. I can't think of anything.

Therapist: Well, I'll help you start. Didn't you tell me that you generally did well on exams in both high school and college? That you can't remember ever failing a test in either high school or college? Wouldn't that be evidence that you can pass the test?

Luke: Yeah, I did pretty well in high school. I did okay on tests in high school and college.

Therapist: What else?

Luke: Well, I was on the wrestling team in high school and my first few years of college, and I did pretty well there. That was one place I succeeded.

Therapist: Okay. (Writes.) What else?

Luke: Well, I guess even though I've moved from job to job, when I like what I'm doing I do pretty well. I just haven't found the right job, you know?

Therapist: Right. Most of the time you've moved to try to better yourself, not because you've failed.

Luke: I think being a police officer is really what I want, if I can ever pass the test.

Therapist: What other evidence do you have that you can pass the test?

Luke: Well, I'm to the point now where most of the time I'm passing practice tests. I never got to that point last time I took the test.

Therapist: Yes, that's good evidence. (Writes.) What else?

Luke: I guess that I'm not drinking now, like before. The fact that I'm not drinking is evidence that I might pass this time, because last time when I failed I was drinking a lot and it interfered with my studying.

Go on this way until the patient has covered all the evidence for and against the automatic thought. It is a good idea to begin with evidence that reflects negatively on the patient, then end by evaluating evidence that reflects positively. This way you and the patient end the exercise on an upbeat note.

You can ask patients to fill out the Re-Rate Emotions column after completing the examining the evidence exercise. This way they can see how much doing the exercise altered their feelings.

An important point here is that you are not trying to get the patient to think in a falsely positive manner. Rather, your goal is to get the patient to see the situation as accurately as possible. Then, if there are problems (e.g., continually failing a test), your goal is to help the patient correct behaviors that might be causing the problems.

Generating Alternatives

The patient's automatic thoughts represent one interpretation of events; there are others. Before assuming any one interpretation is correct, we ask the patient to consider all the possibilities and to generate alternative hypotheses to his or her automatic thoughts.

Here is an example from a session with Luke. Luke had brought in a daily mood log about an event from the past week. He had run into an ex-girlfriend named Nicole, who was now married. Nicole was with her two small daughters.

> *Therapist:* What were your automatic thoughts?
> *Luke:* (Reads.) "Nicole didn't want to talk to me."
> *Therapist:* And what were your feelings?
> *Luke:* (Reads). "Rejected," and the intensity was "80."
> *Therapist:* Okay, that's one interpretation of what happened. Nicole didn't want to talk to you. Let's generate some alternatives. Let's talk about what happened and think of some other interpretations.
> *Luke:* Well, what happened was that I ran into Nicole, and we said "Hi" and talked for a minute, and then she rushed off.

Therapist: Right. So let's generate a list of interpretations of what happened. One is the one you picked, that Nicole didn't want to talk to you. What are some others?

Luke: What are some others? Well, I don't know, I guess another one would be that she was in a hurry for some reason.

Therapist: Right. Good. Another one would be that she was in a hurry, late for an appointment or something, maybe something to do with her kids. What are some others?

Luke: Hmm. Another one would be that she was embarrassed. That's because her kids started fighting a little when we stopped to talk. Maybe she was embarrassed at how her kids were behaving or just wanted to get them going because they were acting up.

Keep going this way until the two of you have generated a list of plausible alternative explanations for the events reported in the patient's automatic thoughts.

Depressive thinking is rigid in its negativity. When patients step back and generate alternative interpretations of an upsetting situation, this process counters their rigidity. In many instances, none of the alternative hypotheses can be proven; however, increasing patients' awareness of other possibilities gives them a sense of the full picture, and also demonstrates their own focus on the negative aspects of the situation.

Assign Homework

The homework is to continue filling out Thought Record forms, with the addition of examining the evidence and generating alternatives in the Rational Response column. The patient should fill out the Re-Rate Emotions column after composing the rational response to measure the effect on mood.

In addition, the patient should continue following activity schedules.

Ask for Feedback about the Session

Ask patients if they have anything they would like to say about the session. Empathize with whatever patients say and validate their feelings. If patients express negative affect about the session, help them identify their automatic thoughts, and then together examine the evidence and generate alternative explanations.

SESSION 4

- Set the agenda
- Review homework
  - Cognitive distortions
  - Introduction of appropriate behavioral treatment
- Assign homework
- Ask for feedback about the session

Set the Agenda

Briefly list the topics you wish to cover this session, and ask patients whether they have agenda items they would like to add. Write down the list of agenda items.

Review Homework

Review the past week's homework assignments. Acknowledge the patient for completing assignments. Address any problems and note the positive consequences.

Cognitive Distortions

A good way to present the cognitive distortions is to lay one of the patient's thought records on a table between you so you both can see it during the discussion (or each of you can hold a copy). Try to use one of the patient's records from the preceding week, so the material is fresh in the patient's mind.

Tell the patient: "Beck noticed that depressed patients tend to make certain cognitive errors that serve to keep them depressed. Since depression makes you prone to making these errors, we want you to learn to watch for them, to identify when you are making them, and to correct them. This will help you interpret reality more accurately and give you more control over the depression."

Give the patient the list of cognitive distortions (the Cognitive Distortions handout, see Appendix I. The handout presents a simplified version of the cognitive distortions outlined by Beck).

> *Therapist:* Let's go through the distortions one by one. The first one is "black-or-white thinking." That's when you see things in terms of black or white, with no shades of gray—like, "If I'm not perfect, then I'm a total failure," "If I'm not totally good, then I'm all bad." Do you see what I mean?
>
> *Luke:* Yeah, I think so.
>
> *Therapist:* Looking at your thought record, do you see any black-and-white thinking?
>
> *Luke:* Well, here where I'm thinking about failing the exam, I write that I'm a total loser. That's kind of black-and-white.
>
> *Therapist:* Right. That's a good example. You are either a loser or a winner, there's no middle ground. So where you wrote that automatic thought, you can identify that you're making an error of "black-or-white thinking," and you could write that in the Rational Response column.
>
> Let's look at the second one. That's "overgeneralizing." Overgeneralizing is erroneously assuming that the specifics of one case are true of other cases. For example, if you fail one test, you say to yourself that you fail at everything you do. Do you see?
>
> *Luke:* Yeah. My mother was a great one for that. You'd do one thing, like break a dish or get the floor dirty, and there she'd be, "Luke, you always make such a

mess, you're always so clumsy." "Always" was her favorite word.

Therapist: Well, then you see where you learned to overgeneralize, from your mother.

Luke: And come to think of it, she was pretty depressed a lot of the time, too. Maybe I'm depressed because my mother was. She was always so negative.

Therapist: It's very possible that you learned to think the way you do from your mother. But rather than discussing that right now, let's continue reviewing the cognitive distortions. Learning to change your negative thinking will help you more now than understanding how your mother influenced your depression. Does that sound okay to you?

Luke: Yeah, that sounds okay.

Therapist: Then let's look at the third one, "focusing on the negative."

Keep going this way until you have covered all the cognitive distortions on the handout. Where appropriate, ask the patient to give examples of the various distortions, preferably from the patient's own thought records.

Tell patients that their homework for the following week is to study their automatic thoughts and identify any cognitive distortions. They should list the cognitive distortions they identify in the Rational Response column, and then re-rate their feelings in the Re-Rate Emotions column.

Introduction of Appropriate Behavioral Treatment

Depending on the patient's specific issues, select a behavioral treatment from the second part of this book and introduce it to the patient.

Assign Homework

The homework is to continue self-monitoring of automatic thoughts, with the addition of listing the cognitive distortions in the Rational Response column. The patient should continue examining the evidence and generating alternatives in the Rational Response column as well.

In addition, the patient should have homework related to the behavioral treatment covered in this session, and should continue following agreed-upon activity schedules.

Ask for Feedback about the Session

Ask patients if they have anything they would like to say about the session. If patients express negative affect about the session, help them to become aware of their automatic thoughts, and, if relevant, to identify any cognitive distortions.

SESSION 5

- Set the agenda
- Review homework
  - Hypothesis testing
  - Problem solving
  - Continuing appropriate behavioral treatment
- Assign homework
- Ask for feedback about the session

Set the Agenda

Briefly list the items you wish to cover in this session, and ask patients whether they have any items they wish to add to the agenda.

Review Homework

Review the past week's homework assignments. Address any problems and point out the positive consequences of doing the homework.

Hypothesis Testing

Hypothesis testing is setting up an experiment to test a hypothesis.

> *Therapist:* The next cognitive technique we want you to do in the Rational Response column is called hypothesis testing. This means to take one of the hypotheses you see in your automatic thoughts and to set up a way to test it.

Let's look at an example. Let's look at the Thought Record form you filled out this morning. The trigger was, "I woke up this morning dreading studying." Here are your automatic thoughts. Will you read them aloud?

Luke: (Reads.) "I can't stand this anymore. It's all a waste. I'm just going to fail anyway. I feel like I'm not making any progress."

Therapist: What is the hypothesis you're making there?

Luke: That I'm not making any progress and I'm going to fail?

Therapist: Right. Exactly. Your hypothesis is that you're not making any progress in your studying for the exam and therefore you are going to fail. Can you think of a way to test that? How could you test whether or not you are making progress?

Luke: How could I test whether or not I'm making progress? I don't know.

Therapist: What do you have that tells you how you're doing?

Luke: Well, I have my practice tests.

Therapist: How many do you have?

Luke: I've taken eight so far.

Therapist: How have you done?

Luke: I'd have to go back and look. But I failed the first couple, you know that. Lately I haven't failed.

Therapist: Can you see a way to test whether you're making progress by looking at your practice tests?

Luke: Yeah, I could look at them and see if my scores are going up.

Therapist: Maybe you could do that for homework this week. Sit down and make a list of your scores, put them in chronological order, and see if the scores go up over time. Would that tell you whether your hypothesis is true or false, that you're not making progress?

Luke: Yeah. I could accept that. If the scores are going up, I guess I'm making progress.

In the above example, the therapist's questioning of the patient is a good illustration of "guided discovery." Rather than telling the patient how to test the hypothesis, the therapist asked a series of questions that helped the patient uncover the answer himself. This approach teaches the patient a process for dealing with a negative thinking pattern, rather than having to rely on the therapist to correct it.

Go through several examples with the patient. Select one or two for the patient to carry out for homework. Ask the patient to make specific predictions about each hypothesis test. Write them down. In the next session you can discuss whether the predictions came true.

One hypothesis test you can carry out with the patient is a test of whether the patient's depression is improving. You can instruct the patient to complete a Beck Depression Inventory in the session, and compare the score with the score obtained in the first week of treatment. If the patient's depression has improved, great! If not, discuss what about the treatment might need to be modified. Once again, take a problem-solving approach to dealing with difficulties.

Problem Solving

More often than not, when depressed patients subject their automatic thoughts to logical principles and empirical testing, they find out their hypotheses are either false or greatly exaggerated. Seeing this, they feel better.

However, sometimes their hypotheses are correct. Sometimes, rather than negatively distorting reality, the patient is identifying a real problem that requires a real solution. In that case, patients can best view their task as having a problem to solve, and we can teach them techniques of problem solving.

The pessimistic thinking style that accompanies depression interferes with patients' ability to problem solve—depressed patients tend to view situations as overwhelming and hopeless. By elaborating the problem-solving process, the therapist provides patients with a strategy to offset this pessimistic thinking style.

The steps of problem solving are as follows. Write them down and place them in the patient's Mastering Depression Notebook.

1. *Brainstorming solutions:* This means generating as many solutions as possible without stopping to evaluate them. Encourage the patient to be creative and thorough.
2. *Looking at the pros and cons of the solutions:* List the advantages and disadvantages of each proposed solution.
3. *Choosing the best solution and carrying it out:* Consider the importance of the various pros and cons. Pick the solution that seems best and take concrete steps to carry it out.

Here is an example from a session with Luke:

Therapist: Let's look at a problem you're having now in your life as an example and use the problem-solving techniques. Looking at your automatic thoughts over the past week, do you see a problem you've identified that we could work on together?

Luke: (Looks through thought records.) What about my sister being mad at me for not showing up at her barbecue? That's not just distorted thinking, she really is mad at me. My mother told me.

Therapist: Yes, I remember. Thinking your sister is mad at you is not a distortion. She really is mad. Let's use it for the problem-solving exercise.

The first step is generating as many possible solutions to the problem as you can. Don't stop to evaluate how good each solution is, just think of as many as you can.

Luke: I guess one solution would be to apologize.

Therapist: Good. You could apologize to your sister. (Writes it down.) What else? What other solutions can you think of?

Luke: Well, I could do what I usually do, and ignore it and just hope it goes away.

Therapist: Right. That would be another possible solution. You could ignore the situation. (Writes.) What else?

Luke: I could ask my mother to talk to my sister about it.

Therapist: Good. (Writes.) Can you think of anything else?

Continue this way until you have a substantial list, one that includes at least some plausible and constructive solutions. The next step is listing the pros and cons of each solution.

Therapist: (Takes a sheet of paper, makes two columns, writes "pros" and "cons" at the top.) Okay, the first solution you suggested was apologizing. What do you see as the advantages and disadvantages of apologizing to your sister?

Luke: One disadvantage I can think of right away is that doing it will make me uncomfortable. I would rather not.

Therapist: Okay, I'll write that in the "cons" column: "Uncomfortable to do." What else? What other pros and cons do you see?

Luke: Well, one pro would be that I would be taking responsibility for what I did. I wouldn't be running away from my responsibilities.

Therapist: Good. I'll write that in the "pros" column: "It would mean taking responsibility."

Luke: Another pro would be that we'd be talking directly, instead of through my mother. It would be less confusing, less complicated.

Therapist: Good. Another "pro" is: "Would be talking directly to one another, instead of through mother."

Continue until you have listed all the pros and cons of all the proposed solutions.

The next step is to evaluate which solution is best. Discuss the pros and cons the patient has identified. How important is each one? Which are most important?

Therapist: So, let's discuss how important these pros and cons are to you. Let's look through them together, and you can talk about which ones are most important. If you like, you can make a star next to the really important ones.

Luke: Okay.

Therapist: Here's the sheet on the solution of apologizing. (Hands the sheet to Luke.)

Luke: (Reads.) The one about taking responsiblity, that's important to me. I'm tired of seeing myself as a coward who doesn't want to deal with anything. I like the idea of taking responsibility. (Makes a star.)

This one about feeling uncomfortable doing it, that's not as important. If I were to not apologize just because I didn't want to feel uncomfortable, that would make me feel like a weakling, so I don't want my being uncomfortable to be so important. I'm going to put an "x" next to it, because I don't even want it to count.

But keeping things less complicated, keeping my mother out of the middle and dealing with my sister directly, that's pretty important, too. (Makes two stars.)

Go on this way until the patient has explored the importance of the various pros and cons.

Help the patient choose the solution that seems best. Plan together how the patient can take concrete steps to carry it out.

> *Therapist:* So, having done all this, which solution do you think is best?
> *Patient:* (Looking through sheets.) I'd have to say the first one, apologizing. Considering everything, that's the one that feels best to me.
> *Therapist:* I agree. So let's talk about how you can carry it out.
> *Luke:* Okay.

The discussion proceeded into the area of assertiveness training, this session's behavioral treatment.

Continuing Appropriate Behavioral Treatment

The therapist continues the behavioral treatment selected for this session.

Assign Homework

The homework is to continue self-monitoring automatic thoughts, with the addition of hypothesis testing in the Rational Response column. The patient should continue examining the evidence, generating alternatives, and listing the cognitive distortions in the Rational Response column as well.

If, after going through these steps, patients feel they have identified a realistic problem, they should go through the steps of the problem-solving exercise. In addition, the patient should carry out the specific hypothesis tests agreed upon in the session. Finally, the patient will have homework related to the behavioral treatment covered in this session, and should continue following agreed-upon activity schedules.

Ask for Feedback about the Session

Ask patients if they have anything they would like to say about the session. Empathize with whatever patients say and validate their feelings. If patients express negative affect about the session, help them identify their automatic thoughts. If relevant, help the patient construct a hypothesis test or carry out a problem-solving exercise.

SESSION 6

- Set the agenda
- Review homework
  - Identifying and evaluating underlying assumptions and schemas
  - Continuing appropriate behavioral treatment
- Assign homework
- Ask for feedback about the session

Set the Agenda

Briefly list the topics you wish to cover and ask patients if they have any items they would like to add to the agenda.

Review Homework

Review the homework from the past week. Address any problems and reward patients with acknowledgment and by pointing out the positive consequences.

Identifying and Evaluating Underlying Assumptions and Schemas

Up to now we have focused on working with automatic thoughts. However, automatic thoughts are reflections of patients' underlying beliefs about themselves and the world— their schemas. Schemas are core cognitions, emotions, and memories, organized into patterns that tend to recur throughout life. Schemas begin to form early in childhood, based on an interaction between the child's biological temperament and environmental conditions. Schemas can be modified, although the process is considerably more difficult than modifying automatic thoughts.

Help patients identify the negative schemas underlying their automatic thoughts. What themes have emerged in their automatic thoughts? What are their core beliefs about themselves and the world? Do they trust others? Do they expect other people to meet their needs? Do they feel worthy of love? Do they feel capable of functioning independently in the world? Entitled to special treatment?

Young (1990) has proposed a typology that you can use to identify patients' early maladaptive schemas. Thus far he has identified eighteen schemas in five realms, as follows:

Disconnection and Rejection

1. Abandonment/instability
2. Mistrust/abuse
3. Emotional deprivation
4. Defectiveness/shame
5. Social isolation/alienation

Impaired Autonomy and Performance

6. Dependence/incompetence
7. Vulnerability to harm or illness
8. Enmeshment/undeveloped self
9. Failure

Impaired Limits

10. Entitlement/grandiosity
11. Insufficient self-control/self-discipline

Other-Directedness

12. Subjugation
13. Self-sacrifice
14. Approval-seeking/recognition-seeking

Overvigilance and Inhibition

15. Negativity/vulnerability to error
16. Overcontrol/emotional inhibition
17. Unrelenting standards/hypercriticalness
18. Punitiveness

(See Appendix I for a more detailed list by Dr. Young, to which you can refer for help in identifying your patient's schemas.)

These schemas are negative patterns or themes that start in childhood and repeat through life. Especially in more severe cases, schemas are highly emotionally charged: when a schema is triggered the patient is filled with negative affect, such as rage, grief, self-hate, shame, or fear. These schemas are presented (as "lifetraps") in the self-help book *Reinventing Your Life* (Young and Klosko 1993).

Early maladaptive schemas almost always begin in childhood as adaptations to destructive environments. (The earlier a schema forms, the more power it has to shape a life.) The child is abused, abandoned, neglected, emotionally deprived, criticized, dominated—or pampered and spoiled. When childhood ends, the person keeps repeating the pattern. The schemas cause the person to misinterpret reality, or to keep arranging reality so the schema becomes true. Although the schemas made sense in childhood, in adulthood they are self-destructive; they keep the person trapped in the psychological circumstances of childhood, repeating the same self-defeating patterns.

Schemas are strong. They fight for survival. Patients must struggle hard and long to overcome them. It is not realistic to expect patients to overcome their negative schemas in this eight-session treatment. However, you can start them on their way, encouraging them to continue on their own after treatment ends. (Patients can use *Reinventing Your Life* as a guide through this process.)

Overcoming Early Maladaptive Schemas

There are several steps you can take in working to change patients' maladaptive negative schemas (Young 1990). Write the steps in the patient's Mastering Depression Notebook.

1. Identify the negative schema
2. Examine the origins
3. Examine the evidence
4. How rational is the schema?
5. Examine the negative consequences in the patient's adult life
6. Come up with a plan for battling the schema

1. Identify the negative schema Identifying a maladaptive negative schema is the first step toward changing it. Although the schema exerts a powerful influence on the patient's life, often the patient is only vaguely aware of it. Help the patient identify one of his or her core schemas.

Therapist: Let's talk about the themes that run through your automatic thoughts, that are continuing sources of pain and depression for you.

One theme we've talked about a lot is your feeling that you're not good enough. You feel like you're not good enough in your social life, and you feel like you're not good enough in your work life. Because of this you expect people to criticize you and dislike you. Do you know what I mean?

Luke: Yeah. I know I'm like that. I'm insecure, I guess.

Therapist: Let's write that in your Mastering Depression Notebook. Let's write that one of your negative schemas is that you feel like you're not good enough.

If the patient has several of the schemas (which is frequently the case), pick the most central one or two. Try to keep things simple and clear. *Reinventing Your Life* has short questionnaires to help patients identify their schemas.

2. *Examine the origins* Briefly discuss the origins in the patient's childhood. Help the patient see that the negative schema developed for a reason.

Therapist: Do you have any idea why you feel this way? Did you feel this way as a child?

Luke: I've always felt this way.

Therapist: What was happening when you were a child to make you feel not good enough?

Luke: The first thing that comes to mind is my brother. He was such a star. Compared to him I was nothing but a disappointment. My parents treated us like day and night, with him as day and me as night.

Therapist: So as a child you felt not good enough compared to your brother. Let's write that in your notebook. Let's list the origins of your schema in your notebook and put that as number one. (Writes.)

What other factors besides having this star of a brother made you feel not good enough as a child?

Luke: Well, my mother was certainly hard to please. It seemed like she was always criticizing me, always putting down what I did as not good enough. I still feel that way with her.

> *Therapist:* Let's write that as number two: your mother was critical of you.

Continue this way until you have a list of the significant childhood origins of the patient's negative schema.

3. Examine the evidence List all the evidence for and against the schema.

> *Therapist:* Is it true that you're not good enough?
> *Luke:* Yeah, it feels true.
> *Therapist:* What evidence do you have?
> *Luke:* My main evidence is that my brother was better than me at everything. He was great in sports, he was popular. I'm not imagining it, believe me it was true. And also, my parents preferred him over me. It seemed like everyone preferred him over me.
> *Therapist:* So your main evidence is that your brother was better in sports and more popular than you, and your parents preferred him. Do you have any other evidence, either from childhood or now?

Gather all the evidence for and against the schema, writing it down with the patient on a list.

4. How rational is the schema? Together with the patient, evaluate the validity of the patient's schema. Considering the evidence, does it make logical sense?

> *Therapist:* Let's look at how reasonable your schema is. What about it? How reasonable is your belief that you're not good enough? Let's go through the steps together.
>
> First, there is generating alternatives. What are some alternative explanations for what happened to

you as a child, other than that you just weren't good enough? What else might explain what your situation was in your family, with your brother being the star and your parents preferring him?

Luke: Well, maybe another explanation is that my brother was more like them, social and athletic, whereas I was different. I was quieter, more shy.

Therapist: Yes, that's a good alternative explanation. You were different than they were. They were more extroverted, and you were more introverted.

Go through all the cognitive therapy steps: generating alternatives, checking for cognitive distortions, hypothesis testing, and problem solving (if necessary).

Write a flash card that summarizes what the patient learns. The patient can carry around the flash card and read it whenever the schema is triggered.

5. Examine the negative consequences in the patient's adult life Generate a list of the schema's negative consequences in the patient's current life, and put the list in the Mastering Depression Notebook. Reading the list will help the patient sustain the motivation to keep battling the schema after treatment ends.

Therapist: What are the consequences of your belief that you're not good enough? What does the schema do to your life?

Luke: It makes me lose confidence, that's for sure. It makes me a nervous wreck.

Therapist: Let me write that as number one. Thinking that you're not good enough makes you lose confidence and makes you a nervous wreck. (Writes.)
What else?

Luke: It's got a lot to do with my drinking, actually. When I'm out and I start feeling not as good as everyone else, *that* makes me want to have a drink.

Therapist: Let's write that as number two: thinking that you're not good enough makes you want to drink. (Writes.)

Keep going this way until you have a list of the schema's negative consequences in the patient's current life.

6. Come up with a plan for battling the schema Write the plan in the patient's notebook. It will serve as a source of homework assignments for the coming year. The plan should be a set of goals for fighting the schema. For example, here are some of the goals Luke set (with the help of his therapist):

1. Fill out a Thought Record whenever the schema "I'm not good enough" is triggered.
2. Whenever the schema is triggered, connect the way I'm feeling with the way I felt in childhood.
3. When I talk to other people, don't put myself down in any way. Fight against any negative thoughts that come into my mind.
4. Be assertive with my mother when she criticizes me.
5. Date women who are supportive, not critical.
6. Be more honest about who I am with my family and friends. Stop lying.
7. Stop criticizing other people.
8. Stop comparing myself to my brother. Whenever I notice myself doing it, do a "stop and switch" to something else in my mind.

Place the list of goals in the patient's Mastering Depression Notebook. The patient can refer to the list for ideas about self-help homework assignments after treatment ends.

Continuing Appropriate Behavioral Treatment

The therapist continues the behavioral treatment selected for this session.

Assign Homework

Tell patients that the homework for the coming week is to read through the materials on schemas in their Mastering Depression Notebook. If they think of any additional points, they can write them in the notebook. For inspiration, they can begin reading *Reinventing Your Life*.

In addition, give patients a specific homework assignment derived from their plan for battling the schema.

Finally, patients should have homework based on the behavioral treatment covered in this session.

Ask for Feedback about the Session

Ask patients if they have anything they would like to say about the session. Empathize with whatever patients say and validate their feelings. If patients express negative affect about the session, help them identify any schema that might have been triggered, and tie the schema to its childhood origins. Help patients verbalize a healthy response to the voice of the schema.

SESSION 7

- Set the agenda
- Review homework
  - Summary of the steps of cognitive therapy
  - Relapse prevention (for treatment responders)
  - Continuing appropriate behavioral treatment
- Assign homework
- Ask for feedback about the session

Set the Agenda

Briefly present the items you wish to cover and ask patients if they have any items they wish to cover.

Review Homework

Review the past week's homework. Address any problems and note the positive consequences.

Summarize the Steps of Cognitive Therapy

Give the patient the form The Steps to Constructing a Rational Response (see Appendix I). Patients can use this form to construct a rational response to their automatic thoughts. It summarizes all the cognitive steps covered in this treatment. This form should be used in addition to the Thought Record as a guide to filling out the Rational Response column. Practice filling one out with the patient, preferably using a situation that is currently upsetting.

Relapse Prevention (for Treatment Responders)

Treatment Responders

Treatment responders are patients who have shown the following:

1. *Clinically significant improvement in their depression:* The patient is no more than mildly depressed (i.e., has a score of less than 10 on the Beck Depression Inventory), and does not display any signs or symptoms of suicidality.
2. *Improvement in social and occupational functioning:* The patient no longer shows significant impairment in social and occupational functioning (due to depression or another mental disorder).

These patients can move into the phase of relapse prevention.

Relapse prevention Since many—perhaps most—patients with depression have relapses, it is important to motivate them to continue using treatment strategies once regular therapy sessions end. Help patients build coping skills for managing future occurrences of depression. The essential point is that they regard the reappearance of depressive symptoms as a cue to start actively coping, rather than catastrophizing and sinking back into depression.

Work out a plan for patients to follow that immediately involves their becoming active. Place the plan in the Mastering Depression Notebook. Get a commitment from patients to follow the plan whenever they experience symptoms of depression that are mild or stronger.

Therapist: When you think about treatment ending, what are your thoughts and feelings?

Luke: I worry about what will happen if I start to get depressed again.

Therapist: What would you want to happen?

Luke: I guess that I remember what I learned here in some way and that I can do something about it. The thought of getting that depressed again scares me. It scares me to think that it could happen to me again.

Therapist: Let's make a plan together for what you could do if you start getting depressed. Let's put it in your notebook so that you have it if you need it after treatment ends.

Write the plan in your handwriting. Include all the components of the patient's treatment.

Therapist: What do you think should be the first step of the plan? Imagine that it's sometime after treatment, and you notice you're getting depressed. What do you think you should do first?

Luke: Well, I guess I could start doing my thought records.

Therapist: Yes, starting to self-monitor is an excellent idea. I'll write that down. (Writes.)

If you start to get depressed again, I want you to remember that your immediate goal is to feel better. I don't want you to worry about anything else until you feel better. How could you do that? Would you be willing to start scheduling pleasurable activities again?

Luke: Yeah. That's a good idea. I could do that.

Therapist: So I'll write that down, too. (Writes.)

Luke: I could listen to my tape if I feel depressed.

Therapist: Yes, that's good, I'll write that as number three: "Listen to your relaxation tape."

Keep going until you cover everything the patient learned in the course of treatment. It is important to make the list concrete. If and when patients become depressed again, it might be hard for them to generate concrete examples on their own.

When the patient should seek help again Help patients define when it is necessary to seek help for depression again. Write the criteria in the patient's Mastering Depression Notebook in terms the patient can understand. Give the patient several copies of the Beck Depression Inventory to put in the notebook as well.

The patient should seek help again if any of the following are true:

1. The patient experiences moderate depression (i.e., a score of 10 or greater on the Beck Depression Inventory) nearly every day for two weeks.
2. The patient has persistent suicidal thoughts or feelings that he or she would rather be dead.
3. The patient is experiencing significant impairment in social or occupational functioning (e.g., not socializing with friends, having trouble completing work) due to depression or another mental disorder.

Encourage patients to deal with their depression *early* and *actively.* We hope that they will use the techniques they have learned in treatment to keep their depression at low levels. However, if they try to manage their depression on their own and they fail, they should seek help again.

This is an intermittent treatment model in which the therapist minimizes patients' dependence and patients learn to cope on their own. Many patients who have responded well to treatment will be able to maintain their benefits independently for long periods of time.

Treatment Nonresponders

Treatment nonresponders are patients who, at this point in treatment, meet any of the following three criteria:

1. They are at least moderately depressed (i.e., a score of 10 or greater on the Beck Depression Inventory).
2. They display signs or symptoms of suicidality.
3. They display significant impairment in social or occupational functioning (due to depression or another mental disorder).

Patients who meet any of these three criteria at this point in treatment will not be ready to terminate at the end of eight sessions. They will require continued treatment. These patients will not move into the phase of relapse prevention, nor will they complete the material we present in Session 8 on maintenance and generalization. Rather, the disposition of these cases must be determined on a case-by-case basis.

Continuing Appropriate Behavioral Treatment

The therapist continues the behavioral treatment selected for this session.

Assign Homework

For treatment responders, the homework is to think about termination. What questions does the patient have? What concerns? Tell the patient to write down any thoughts in the Mastering Depression Notebook, and to bring the notebook to the next session.

In addition, the patient should have homework based on the behavioral treatment covered in this session.

Ask for Feedback about the Session

Ask patients if they have anything they would like to say about the session. Empathize with whatever they say and validate their feelings. If they express negative affect about the session, help them identify their automatic thoughts, and together fill out the form The Steps to Constructing a Rational Response.

SESSION 8

- Set the agenda
- Review homework
  - Plan for maintenance and generalization
  - Termination

Set the Agenda

List what you wish to discuss and ask patients if they have any items they would like to add.

Review Homework

Review the homework from the past week.

Plan for Maintenance and Generalization

Together think about the patient's short-term and long-term goals. Write them down on two lists, one for the next six months, and the other for the patient's future life. Put the lists in the Mastering Depression Notebook.

Here is the list of Luke's goals for the six months following the end of treatment.

1. Pass my police exam.
2. Go to AA meetings twice a week.
3. Do at least one pleasurable activity per day.
4. Fill out a self-monitoring form every time I have a negative feeling that is 50 or greater on a 0 to 100 scale (with 50 being moderate).
5. Do a relaxation technique whenever I feel stressed (50 or greater on a 0 to 100 scale).

6. Review my Mastering Depression Notebook at least once a month.
7. Every week give myself a homework assignment (hypothesis testing, assertiveness, relaxation, fighting my "I'm not good enough" schema).
8. Review highlighted sections of *Feeling Good* once per month. Keep reading and carrying out the exercises in *Reinventing Your Life*.

Luke's list of life goals (again, written in the therapist's handwriting and placed in his Mastering Depression Notebook) was as follows:

1. Keep fighting my "I'm not good enough" schema.
2. Become a police officer.
3. Let people who really care about me (my sister, my friends) get closer to me.
4. Be assertive at all times, not passive and not aggressive.
5. Keep my body relaxed under stress.
6. Deal with my depression as soon as it becomes a problem.
7. Give myself a homework assignment every week to work on my life.
8. Keep moving toward getting married and having children. Someday be a good husband and father.

Termination

Encourage patients to say everything they have to say about termination. Invite them to explore all their feelings. Empathize with their feelings. Validate the patient. Share your feelings (when you know they will have a positive effect on the patient). Together review the progress the patient has made.

Help the patient feel you are always there in some way. This is ultimately the function of the Mastering Depression Notebook: it is a link to you and to what the patient has learned in these sessions. Write your name and your telephone numbers in the notebook. Remind patients that they can meet with you again if they have the need. If you feel comfortable doing so, tell patients to write to you occasionally and say that you will write back.

Remind patients that the termination of therapy is not the end of the change process; it is the beginning, not the end, of change. If patients keep practicing the techniques they have learned in treatment, they will continue to improve.

III

BEHAVIORAL TREATMENTS

This part of the book presents behavioral treatment approaches to a number of problems that often co-occur with depression, such as interpersonal problems, stress-management problems, low productivity, and excessive anxiety. We suggest that you select the treatments that are most applicable to the patient you are treating with our program. The treatments are as follows:

1. Assertiveness training
2. Anger management
3. Relaxation techniques
4. Improving productivity
5. Managing panic attacks
6. Managing worry

ASSERTIVENESS TRAINING

It is rare to meet a depressed patient who does not have assertiveness issues. Depression contributes to both passivity and aggressiveness, the two major obstacles to behaving in appropriately assertive ways. Circularly, both passivity and aggressiveness serve to maintain depression. People who are excessively passive do not express their preferences or ask to have their needs met, and chronically failing to express oneself and get one's needs met fosters depression. At the other extreme, people who are excessively aggressive push others away and tend to wind up disconnected and alone, which likewise fosters depression.

Assertiveness training teaches patients more constructive ways to express their feelings and present their needs, ways that appropriately balance the need for self-respect with the need to respect others.

Education about Assertiveness

The therapist should present the idea that there is a continuum from passive to aggressive, with assertiveness lying in the middle. Both ends of the continuum are problematic.

Continuum
Passive . . . Assertive . . . Aggressive

At the passive end, the person places too little value on the needs and rights of the self and too much on the needs and rights of the other person.

> *Therapist:* When you are being passive, you do not express your needs. You do not try to get your needs met. Rather, your whole goal is meeting the needs of the other person. You don't talk, you *listen.* You submit to whatever you think the other person wants, even if it involves a loss of self-esteem. In your effort to respect the other person, you forget to respect yourself.

At the aggressive end, the person places too little value on the needs and rights of the other person and too much on the needs and rights of the self.

Therapist: When you are being aggressive, you do not consider the needs of the other person. Rather, your whole goal is meeting your own needs. You do not consider the rights of the other person. Your goal is making sure your own rights are taken into account, even if it's at the expense of the other person. You don't listen, you *talk.* You dominate and bully to get your way. In your effort to make sure you are respected, you forget to respect the other person.

Midway between passivity and aggression lies assertiveness. Here, the person places equal value on the needs and rights of the self and the needs and rights of the other person.

Therapist: When you are being assertive, your goal is reciprocity and balance. You try to treat both yourself and the other person with respect.

This is the central idea of assertiveness: Always be respectful to yourself and always be respectful to the other person.
Make the distinction for the patient between content and presentation in attempts to communicate. Assertiveness is not about content, it is about presentation.

Therapist: Assertiveness is not about *what* you are saying; it is about *how* you are saying it. No matter what you are trying to say, it is always possible to express yourself assertively.

It is a common pattern for patients to swing from one pole to the other on the assertiveness continuum. That is, the patient may be excessively passive in one devaluing situation after another and then suddenly swing to the opposite pole and fly into a rage over some seemingly minor matter, then, in remorse, sink back into excessive passivity and start the cycle again.

> *Therapist:* For example, you might have a friend who continually makes little digs at you. You may take it and take it and take it, and then one time explode with anger at one of his digs. From the outside it might look as though you overreacted, and it may even feel like an overreaction to you. But your reaction makes more sense when you consider that you are not just expressing anger for this one incident but for all the other times it happened, too.
>
> Alternatively, you may be aggressive for a period of time, and then swing to the opposite pole of passivity. This is a common pattern in abusive relationships. Following a period of abuse the abuser becomes contrite and excessively meek, holding in anger whenever it occurs. The anger builds to a breaking point, and then the abuse starts all over again.

Another common pattern is to be passive-aggressive.

> *Therapist:* This means to appear passive but actually to be aggressive. For example, say your friend asks you for a favor that you consider excessive and unreasonable. You feel angry at your friend and you want to say no. If you were to handle this situation passive-aggressively, you would say yes and then not follow through. You would forget, or bungle the favor somehow, or do it too late. On the surface you would seem affable and willing, but in fact you would be expressing anger at the friend by not following through with the request.

Help patients identify their own pattern. Pick a situation in their current lives that typifies this pattern, and use it as an example throughout the assertiveness training. If you illustrate each point you make with an actual situation from their lives, patients will relate better to the assertiveness material.

Building Motivation: Looking at the Consequences

To help the patient build the motivation to attempt change, examine the negative consequences of passivity and aggression. Focus most on the consequences of the patient's own style.

> *Therapist:* The main negative consequence of the passive style is unhappiness. You don't ask for what you want or get what you need, your rights get trampled constantly, and you have to cope with a growing sense of resentment simmering underneath the surface. Naturally this resentment contributes to your depression.
>
> The main negative consequence of the aggressive style is unhappiness as well. This is because your aggressiveness costs you a great deal. It costs you emotionally—it pushes people away, even (or especially!) the ones you love most. After a while the people closest to you leave you or retaliate. And it costs you in other ways, as you lose jobs, get into arguments or fights, cause friends to dislike socializing with you, or otherwise pay for being a bully.

Help patients explore the negative consequences of their particular style. Write down the list in the patient's Mastering Depression Notebook. Make a flash card that summarizes the reasons to change. Tell patients to carry around the card and to read it whenever they are trying to remember why it is important to work on their assertiveness skills.

Building Assertiveness Skills

Learning the Principles of Assertiveness

Give the patient the handout The Principles of Assertiveness (see Appendix I). Present the principles of assertiveness by reviewing the handout together.

> *Therapist:* Let's look at the first principle. The overarching goal of any assertiveness exercise is to respect yourself and the other person equally. When you evaluate how you did afterwards, these are the questions to ask yourself: Did I maintain my self-respect? Did I respect the other person?
>
> The handout lists some criteria you can use to evaluate your performance. First we have the "do's" of assertiveness. These are guidelines for becoming less passive. As you can see, it says, if you truly want to, to express your feelings, ask for what you need, state your preferences, and assert your rights.
>
> The next set of guidelines will help you behave less aggressively. These are the "don'ts" of assertiveness, and they include: don't yell, don't hit or otherwise physically dominate or intimidate the person, don't call the person names or otherwise attack him personally, don't say things simply to hurt the person, and don't lose control of your anger.
>
> Let's look at the second assertiveness principle. It's "define your goal." Before you carry out an assertiveness exercise, think it through. What are you try-

ing to accomplish? Be clear within yourself about your goals.

The third principle is to choose an appropriate setting. Try to choose a time and place that gives you privacy, quiet, peace—whatever setting will most help you achieve your assertiveness goals.

Fourth, try to choose a time when the other person is calm. Try your best to pick a time when the other person is maximally receptive to what you have to say.

Fifth, stay calm yourself. Don't lose control of your anger. If you feel you're going to lose control, leave the situation until you can handle it calmly. (For more on this, see Anger Management below.)

Sixth, use assertive body language. Stand up straight, look the other person in the eye, and speak in a clear and audible voice.

Seventh, be as brief and as clear as possible. The more brief and clear you are, the more powerful your message will be.

Eighth, talk about your personal feelings, not about objective "rightness." Don't preach to the other person about right and wrong. Rather, speak in a personal way. Use "I feel" statements. Say things like: "I feel angry that you . . . I feel uncomfortable when you . . . I don't like it when you . . ."

Ninth, don't get defensive. Don't overjustify your feelings. Don't start listing all the reasons that explain why you're speaking. Your feelings are enough justification—you do not need to speak of any others.

Tenth, request specific behavior change. Tell the person exactly what you want him to do to correct the situation. Be specific and concrete. Criticize the behavior, not the person. Say, "I don't like it when you throw your clothes on the floor"; not, "You're a slob." Say, "Please start putting them in the hamper or putting them away"; not, "Stop being such a slob."

Eleventh, when you want to say something negative, start and end with something positive. This is the "sandwich technique," so called because you sandwich a negative between two positives. Don't make up the positives: use positives that are true. For example, if you are criticizing someone's performance at work, start and end with examples of the way the person is truly performing well; or, if you are criticizing someone you love, start and end by expressing positive feelings toward the person.

Twelfth, if the other person protests, simply keep restating your position. This principle helps you stay on track and true to your goal. Don't get lost in arguments the other person raises. Don't go off on tangents. Don't retreat because you have trouble tolerating the other person's anger. No matter what the other person says, just calmly and succinctly keep restating your point.

Tell patients to place the handout in their Mastering Depression Notebook. They can use this handout to evaluate their performance whenever they practice assertiveness.

Begin Self-Monitoring and Self-Evaluation

Teach patients how to self-monitor their assertiveness.

Therapist: The cue to self-monitor is any situation in your life that you want to manage in an assertive way. It can be a past situation you want to review and learn from, or it can be a current situation you want to handle well, or it can be a future situation for which you want to prepare.

Whenever any of these come up, self-monitoring will help you stay self-aware and in control. Each time you are confronted with one of these situations, you have an opportunity to build your assertiveness skills.

Expressing an opposing preference or point of view, asking people to change their behavior, refusing unreasonable requests—these are the types of situations that call upon a person to be assertive.

Therapist: Voicing a different opinion than another person, confronting people when they do something you don't like, saying no when you want to say no—these kinds of situations serve as cues for you to begin self-monitoring your assertiveness skills.

Give patients a copy of the Self-Monitoring for Assertiveness form (see Appendix I). Show them how to fill it out. Illustrate each step with an example from their current lives.

Therapist: Let's look at this form together, and I'll explain how to fill it out.

In the first part, where it says, "What is the situation, you describe the situation in one or two sentences: for example, "I called my friend Elizabeth a week ago and

left a message on her machine, and she still hasn't
called me back."

Next, you write down how you *feel* about the situation.
You may have more than one feeling: anger, sadness,
hurt, disappointment, jealousy, sympathy. Look carefully at your feelings and write down all of them.

As you write down each feeling, rate how intense each is
on a 0 to 100 scale. The scale is as follows:

0	25	50	75	100
Not intense	Mild	Moderate	Intense	Very Intense

Next, write down your automatic thoughts about the situation: for example, "She does this to me all the time.
She never calls me back. It makes me feel like she
doesn't really care about me."

Next evaluate your automatic thoughts. Are there errors
in your thinking? Is your thinking in line with the
evidence?

Write a rational response to your thoughts if they are irrational: "Elizabeth doesn't *always* do this, but she
does it a lot. Too much. And I know she really cares.
But I still think her behavior is insensitive and I need
to talk to her about it."

Next, describe your behavior until now and its consequences. What have you done so far? Write this down:
"So far I've done nothing. I just wait for her to call
me. Sometimes I call her back two or three times
before she finally calls. I've never said anything. I'm
nice to her even though I'm mad."

What are the consequences of what you have done so far?
How do you feel inside about it? "I feel frustrated and
angry with Elizabeth and with myself."

Next, write down your goals. What do you want to accomplish? Define your goals: "I want to tell Elizabeth it makes me angry when she doesn't call me back. I want to tell her to start calling me back when I call her."

Remember that your overarching goal is always to behave assertively—to respect both yourself and the other person equally. Do not make changing the other person one of your goals. The other person may or may not change; that is not within your control.

Judge the success of an assertiveness exercise by how well you have behaved. Even if the other person does not change, you can walk away satisfied with yourself if you have behaved in accord with the principles of assertiveness.

Next, describe how you want to behave: the assertive way to meet your goals. Spell out how to handle the situation assertively: for example, "I could arrange a quiet time for us to talk, and calmly tell her that it makes me angry and hurts my feelings when she doesn't return my calls. I could ask her to try to remember to call me back from now on. I could sandwich this between two positive messages about how I care about her and value our friendship."

Rehearsing Assertiveness Exercises

Present the rationale for practicing assertiveness exercises before carrying them out.

Therapist: Once you have filled out your self-monitoring form, you are ready to practice your assertiveness exercise.

Ideally, you should practice until you have the whole thing down pat—until you know just how you want to handle yourself in every possible scenario that might come up.

Considering all possible scenarios is important because you want to be prepared for anything. You want to know exactly how to handle it if the other person responds well or badly.

Remember that how the other person responds is not the important thing. What is important is that you reach your goals and handle yourself well. No matter what the other person does, you can always reach your assertiveness goals.

You and I can rehearse together, here in our sessions. Later, you can rehearse at home.

The two main ways patients can practice assertiveness before undertaking an exercise are imagery and role playing.

Imagery

The patient can use imagery to develop a vision of what behaving assertively means in a situation. The imagery can follow a relaxation induction (see Relaxation Techniques below), or can be done by itself.

Instruct patients to close their eyes and to imagine themselves carrying out the assertiveness exercise. What is the situation? How do they want to behave? Help patients to make the image as vivid as possible.

> *Therapist:* Close your eyes and get an image of yourself telling Elizabeth how you feel about her not calling back. Where are you? What's going on? Tell me what you see.
>
> *Patient:* (Closes eyes.) Well, I see Elizabeth and me, and we're sitting in my backyard.

Therapist: Good. Look around the backyard and tell me what you see. Could you do that?

Patient: Okay. I see the patio and the grass and the flower garden. I see the hedges, and through the hedges I see the backyard of the people who live behind us.

Therapist: Is anyone else there?

Patient: The kids are there, playing. They're playing ball on the lawn.

Therapist: What is the day like? Is it hot and sunny?

Patient: No, it's cool. It's sunny, but cool.

Therapist: And what happens? What do you see?

Patient: Well, I'm waiting for the right time to tell her, for a pause in the conversation. Then a good time comes, and I lean forward, and I tell her that she's one of my best friends, but that I have to tell her that when she doesn't call me back on the phone when I call her it makes me mad at her. I ask her to please try to call me back when I call.

Therapist: And what does she say?

Patient: She says okay.

Therapist: You know her. What else might she say?

Patient: Well, she might say she doesn't mean to hurt my feelings, she just forgets, she's so busy, that kind of thing.

Therapist: And how do you want to handle that?

Patient: I guess I just want to say, "That may be true, but it bothers me, and I want you to try to remember to call me back."

Consider many scenarios in the imagery. What does the patient want to do if the person responds this way, or that way, or in the worst possible way?

When you have finished exploring the assertiveness exercise through imagery, evaluate with patients how well they did. Were the behaviors they imagined appropriately assertive? Did they respect themselves and the other person? Did they fulfill the twelve principles of assertiveness?

Let the patient do most of the talking during this evaluation process. Do not lecture or preach. Focus on praising the good aspects of their imagined performance. Ask patients questions until they themselves are aware of what they did well and what they need to improve.

Role Playing

In addition, you and the patient can role-play the assertiveness exercise. You can play the patient if you want to model assertiveness. However, most of the time you will probably play the other person in the patient's exercise.

Therapist: Why don't we role-play the exercise? I'll play Elizabeth, and you can role-play telling me about the calling.

Patient: Okay.

Therapist: So, let's say I'm Elizabeth, and you and I are sitting in the backyard. And the kids are playing and there's a pause in the conversation. What do you say?

Patient: I say: "Elizabeth, you're one of my best friends, but there's something you do that bothers me. When I call you on the phone you don't call me back."

Therapist: (playing Elizabeth) Oh, well, I don't? Are you sure? You know how busy I get. I know I mean to call you back. I don't mean anything by it, you know that.

Patient: Yes, I know, I know you don't mean to make me upset. But I have to say it still bothers me, and I want you to try to remember to call me back.

Therapist: (as self) You know Elizabeth. What would she say now?

Patient: Um, she would say okay, I think; she would say that she would try.

Therapist: (as Elizabeth) Okay. I'll try to remember.

Do the role play many times, working through many different variations and scenarios. Troubleshoot with patients. Help them polish their performance. Help them become comfortable about carrying out the exercise in real life.

Carrying Out the Assertiveness Exercise
as a Homework Assignment

We hope at this point that the patient will feel ready to carry out the assertiveness exercise. Agree that the patient will carry out the exercise as a homework assignment sometime in the coming week. The patient should fill out a Self-Monitoring for Assertiveness form and bring it to the next session. You and the patient can discuss the results of the exercise at that time.

Patients can adapt the procedures of self-monitoring, rehearsing, and carrying out assertiveness exercises to other situations in their lives.

ANGER MANAGEMENT

Anger problems and depression interact in many different and subtle ways. Anger problems frequently co-occur with depression and are most likely both a cause and a result of depression. Irritability can be a symptom of depression. Other depression symptoms, such as sleep disturbance and low energy, often make the people who experience them irritable. Feelings of helplessness can contribute to anger problems. When depressed people display outbursts of anger, they are often compensating for underlying feelings of helplessness. Further, depressed people tend to produce feelings of irritability in others. Research shows that they are less skillful than non-depressed people in solving interpersonal problems. In conversation with others, depressed people tend to focus on themselves and speak in negative tones. They communicate feelings of sadness, helplessness, and low self-esteem. Finally, the consequences of anger-management problems, such as relationship difficulties and lost work opportunities, decrease the positive reinforcement in people's lives, and thus increase their depression.

The basic components of the anger-management treatment we present are (1) building and sustaining motivation to work on the problem, (2) initiating the use of a time-out procedure, (3) the use of cognitive and somatic self-calming techniques, and (4) responding assertively. We intend readers to use this discussion on anger management in conjunction with the discussion on assertiveness training: anger-management teaches patients self-control over their angry outbursts; assertiveness training teaches them to express their anger in appropriate ways.

Case Example

Rianna is 27 years old. She is moody and emotionally intense. She has come to therapy because she is prone to periods of depression. Anger comes up as an issue at the insistence of her fiancé Jack, who is threatening to call off their marriage unless she does something about her anger.

> *Rianna:* Jack made me promise to bring this up in therapy. He's upset with me. He's upset because when I get mad I yell at him.

Rianna has a bad temper. Although her depression worsens the problem, Rianna does not only have it when she is depressed. She has always had the problem. "I can't help it. It's just the way I am," she says. "I've been this way my whole life." As a child, Rianna yelled at her mother and sister in the same way that she yells at Jack today.

Although Rianna's angry outbursts only last a few minutes, Jack feels shaken and upset for hours afterward, even days. Rianna has yelled at him in public places and in front of friends and family. Once she yelled at him in front of a business client and he nearly broke up with her.

> *Rianna:* I don't know why Jack makes such a big deal out of it. I get mad, I yell, and then it's over. It's not like I stay mad. I never hold a grudge like he does.
> *Therapist:* So do you think your anger is a problem?
> *Rianna:* No, not really.

Rianna feels entitled to yell when she is angry. She has little empathy or understanding about how her outbursts affect others. We ask her how it feels when she yells, and she tells us,

"It feels like I'm right." We ask her what she wants when she yells, and she says, "I want to win."

Many patients come to therapy because they are having trouble managing their emotions. They feel overwhelmed by their feelings—anxiety, grief, guilt, shame, jealousy, hopelessness—and they cannot seem to get control on their own. However, when the issue is anger, patients often do not seek help for this problem. They do not come to therapy, or, if they do come, they do not bring it up. Many more patients have anger problems than try to solve them in therapy. This is not because managing anger is easy. On the contrary, developing effective ways to express anger is one of the greatest challenges in life. Then why do patients rarely seek help for anger-management problems? The answer is simple. Patients are often unmotivated to learn to control their anger.

Anxiety, grief, guilt—these emotions feel bad. They are inherently painful. When they are too intense they drive people into therapy. But anger does not feel bad. It feels good. While patients might regret later what they did when they were angry, at the time, in the moment they express the anger, it feels good. The problem is that it feels bad to the people around them. Moreover, anger is often an effective strategy, at least in the short run. When Rianna yells at Jack in public, he will do anything to quiet her down. He feels embarrassed and intimidated. Most of the time when she loses her temper, Rianna gets what she wants. She "wins." Rianna might win the battles and lose the war, however, especially if Jack leaves her. In the long run, her anger management problems are having a damaging impact on her life.

Rianna is typical of patients with anger problems. She is raising the issue in therapy because she is faced with some terrible consequence of her anger. Many anger-management patients are this way. They are in crisis: their spouses are threatening to leave them, their bosses are threatening to fire them, their children are threatening to stop talking to them. Their anger is ruining something they value, something they do not want to lose. Such potential losses can contribute to their depression.

Building and sustaining motivation is a core issue in teaching patients to control their anger.

Building and Sustaining Motivation

First, patients must accept that managing anger is a problem for them and make a commitment to solve the problem. For the reasons discussed above, this is often the hardest step.

Through directed questioning, guide patients to confront the long-term consequences of their anger—how it is alienating the ones they love, holding them back in their career, damaging friendships, pushing people away.

As you go through this discussion, write a list of these consequences. Afterward, you can give the list to the patient to put in the Mastering Depression Notebook.

> *Therapist:* Let's make a list of the reasons you have for wanting to learn to control your anger. I'll write them down.
>
> What reasons do you have? If you don't learn to control your anger, what will it do to your life? What has it done to your life so far?
>
> *Rianna:* Aside from getting Jack all upset and costing me a couple of roommates in college, I can't think of anything.
>
> *Therapist:* What happened in college?

Rianna: Oh, I was sharing a suite with these two girls, and after the first semester they asked me to move out. This happened right after I got really mad at one of them for eating some of my food. I needed the food for that meal or something, my boyfriend was coming over, I was really upset. Maybe I shouldn't have gotten so mad, but she shouldn't have taken my food!

Therapist: What did you do?

Rianna: Oh, I yelled at her. Nothing major, really.

Therapist: How did you feel when they asked you to move out?

Rianna: Pretty bad, actually. It was a drag. I had to look for a place off-campus. I had to move over my vacation.

Therapist: Did you like the girls?

Rianna: Yeah, I really did. But I didn't see them much after I moved.

Therapist: So that would be one consequence, right? Losing your temper cost you some friends.

Rianna: That's true.

Therapist: So I'll write that down.

Rianna: Okay.

Therapist: The other thing you said was that your anger gets Jack upset. Should we talk about that? What does his being upset do to your life?

Rianna: Well, it sure plays hell with my sex life! (Laughs.) Jack doesn't want to come near me after one of our fights.

Therapist: I know you're laughing, but I also know that it really hurts you when he doesn't want to have sex.

Rianna: I know.

Therapist: Then I'll write that down, too. It damages your sex life with Jack. How else does it affect your relationship with Jack?

Continue until you have as complete and meaningful a list as possible. Tell patients to read the list at least once a day. Suggest that they carry the list around with them and read it whenever they feel at risk of losing control of their anger. Being immediately aware of the concrete consequences of losing control of their anger will motivate them to employ their strategies to control it.

The Steps of Anger Management

Give patients an overview of the three steps of anger management. Write the three steps in their Mastering Depression Notebook.

1. Adopt a time-out procedure.
2. Use somatic and cognitive self-calming techniques.
3. Handle the matter in accord with the principles of assertiveness.

Ask patients to commit to following these three steps whenever they experience anger that is 50 or greater on the following anger scale:

0	25	50	75	100
No anger	Mild anger	Moderate anger	Extreme Anger	As much anger as possible

Whenever their anger reaches 50 or higher on the scale, that is, moderate or greater, that is the cue for patients to begin following the three steps.

Adopt a Time-Out Procedure.

> *Therapist:* Whenever your anger is 50 or higher—moderate or greater—that is your cue to do the first step, giving yourself a time-out. Acknowledge your anger to yourself, but give yourself a time-out *before* you express your anger.
>
> A time-out can mean removing yourself from the situation temporarily, or it can mean staying in the situation but refraining from acting or speaking. In a time-out, you can feel your anger, but you cannot act on it.
>
> Stay in the time-out until you are calm, until your anger is 25 (mild) or less on the anger scale.

For example, Rianna told us about one situation with Jack where they were ordering flowers for their wedding and they had a disagreement. She used the time-out procedure:

> *Rianna:* I got really mad at Jack at the florist's. I felt like he didn't care what I wanted. I was about to yell at him in front of the florist and my mother, and I remembered what I agreed to do. So I told everyone I would be right back, and I went and sat in the ladies' room. I knew if I stayed at the table I wouldn't be able to restrain myself from blowing up at him. So I went to the ladies' room to cool down and think about it.

Use Somatic and Cognitive Self-Calming Techniques

> *Therapist:* You can help yourself calm down in the time-out with somatic and cognitive techniques. Somatic techniques will help you calm your body, and cogni-

tive techniques will help you calm the thoughts that are going through your mind.

In terms of somatic techniques, teach the patient relaxation exercises such as meditation, breathing, and imagery. One simple technique is to count one's breaths, purposely breathing slowly and deeply. (For help designing a relaxation exercise suitable for your patient to use in the time-out, see Relaxation Techniques, below.)

In terms of cognitive techniques, the most important one is thinking through the consequences of losing control. This is a basic principle of impulse control. Between the impulse and the action, the patient must learn to insert *thought*.

> *Therapist:* There are a number of cognitive techniques you can use in the time-out to help yourself calm down. The most important one is this: you must force yourself to consider the consequences of losing control of your anger in the situation. Will it really be to your benefit? If someone you love is involved, will losing your temper strengthen your bond with him, or damage that bond? Do you want to damage this relationship, or do you really value it?
>
> If it is your work, will it help you meet your work goals? Consider the situation and try to put it into perspective. Is what is at stake worth getting so upset about?
>
> Ask yourself how it will affect other people. How will it feel to them? Will it frighten or upset them? How would you feel if someone yelled at you?
>
> You can read the list we wrote together of your reasons for wanting to learn to control your anger. That can help you regain control as well.

Other cognitive techniques the patient can use are filling out a Thought Record and reading a list of coping self-statements you have composed together.

Handle the Matter in Accord with the Principles of Assertiveness

Once patients are calm, they can design an assertive response to the situation (see Assertiveness Training, above), one that balances the need for self-respect with the need to respect the other person and do what is best for the relationship as a whole.

> *Therapist:* When you are too aggressive, you give too little importance to supporting the relationship with the other person. All you care about supporting is your own self-esteem. When you are assertive, you keep these two considerations in balance. You support the relationship *and* you support your self-esteem.
>
> There are guidelines for you to follow if you want to behave assertively. Most important, stay calm. If you cannot present yourself calmly, then do not present yourself at all. Take a time-out.
>
> Behave in ways that respect both parties equally. Do not put yourself down and do not put down the other person. Do not attack or label the other person. Simply state what the person has done that has upset you. Tell the person clearly how you feel about what he or she has done, and what you want instead.
>
> Try to see the other person's point of view, and validate it. Listen as you would want the other person to listen to you. Try to restate the other person's position to make sure you understand, and to let the other person know that you understand.

Patients should consider carefully what their goals are in the situation. Then, they should try to behave strategically, not emotionally, acting to strengthen and maintain their relationships with significant others.

> *Rianna:* While I was in the ladies' room I thought about how it wasn't really so important that I win the fight. Maybe it wasn't really such a big deal that Jack was disagreeing with me about the flowers. Maybe he wasn't trying to control me, maybe he was just saying what he wanted. Anyway, it's more important that I work on my relationship with Jack, on making it better. That's what I really want. I want to stay together, and I want our relationship to be good.

When Rianna came out of the ladies' room, she did not yell at Jack or insult him. Rather, she calmly told him that she felt he was not listening to her, and that this was making her feel like he didn't care about what she wanted. She asked him to listen to her. Jack was sympathetic and he tried to listen better. The end result was that Rianna and Jack felt closer to one another rather than more distant. This result rewarded Rianna's behavior and helped build her motivation for the next time.

The answer to situations that make our patients lose control of anger is almost always assertiveness. Patients often feel frustrated or threatened by a situation, do nothing at first, then explode in anger. Assertiveness training encourages patients to deal directly with situations as they occur and express their needs, rather than waiting for things to build up to unmanageable levels. Patients will find that if they take this approach, both their self-esteem and their relationships with others will improve.

RELAXATION TECHNIQUES

Relaxation training is a useful treatment for symptoms that are central to depression, such as insomnia and agitation, and symptoms that often co-occur, such as the many physical stress disorders. There is a great deal of research showing that these techniques can be helpful in treating such stress symptoms as asthma, headaches, insomnia, irritable bowel and other gastrointestinal problems, panic attacks, generalized anxiety, weight problems, skin problems, chronic pain, high blood pressure, and fatigue. If your patient has any of these symptoms, these techniques can be a useful addition to treatment.

The purpose of relaxation techniques is to center the mind and calm the body. They include such various methods as meditation, relaxation training, imagery exercises, hypnosis, biofeedback, and breathing techniques. Research indicates that what is most helpful about these methods is the focusing of attention that is the common ingredient of all of them.

Before beginning a relaxation program with a patient for physical stress symptoms, it is your responsibility to make sure that the patient has been medically cleared. Consult with the patient's physician to verify that your program is compatible with the patient's medical regimen.

Collaborate with your patient in designing a relaxation program. Tailor the program to the patient's particular symptoms, personality, talents, and needs.

Education about Stress Symptoms

Begin by educating the patient about the symptoms of stress disorders and the various techniques available for treating them. Give the patient the handout Education about Stress Symptoms (see Appendix I), and cover the material on it.

Therapist: This session we are going to focus on helping you learn techniques to deal with stress. Stress symptoms are physical problems affected by psychological stress. The amount of stress in your life and how you manage that stress psychologically have a significant impact on whether the symptoms ever appear in the first place, and, once they appear, how severe they become.

Stressful events are those involving life changes, positive or negative. Getting married, giving birth to a child, graduating from school, starting a job, buying a house—all these are positive events, and all tend to increase the severity of stress symptoms. Certainly negative life events, such as the breakup of a relationship, the illness or death of someone you love, losing your job, failing in business, falling into debt, likewise increase the severity of stress disorders.

Stress attacks your body at its most vulnerable spot. We are all born with certain physical vulnerabilities. Some of us have slow metabolisms and tend to overeat and become overweight in times of stress. Others have sensitive digestive systems and tend to develop ulcers or irritable bowel. Others have fair, delicate skin, and in times of stress break out in rashes or develop eczema. Stress searches out our natural physical vulnerabilities and capitalizes on them.

We can also develop certain physical vulnerabilities over time, through unhealthy habits or exposure to unhealthy environments. As an example of an unhealthy habit, research shows that people who have panic attacks chronically hyperventilate. That is, they have a habit of breathing incorrectly. This habit creates a physical vulnerability that, under stress, manifests in panic attacks. Other unhealthy habits include smoking, drinking excessive amounts of alcohol, having unprotected sex, eating too much junk food, and getting too little fresh air or too little exercise. Examples of unhealthy environmental factors include excessive noise, pollution, overcrowding, and crime.

Use your patient's particular stress symptoms to illustrate the points we're making.

Present the Rationale

Therapist: Although stress is inevitable in life, we are not totally at its mercy. There are things we can do to help ourselves manage our stressors and thereby minimize their effect on our physical well-being. This is what we are going to do today: teach you skills to cope with stress more effectively in order to lessen the severity of your stress symptoms.

There are many self-control techniques you can learn to calm and center your body. These include biofeedback, relaxation training, breathing exercises, meditation, and visualization. Interestingly, all these techniques seem to work in the same way. They teach a *focus of attention*. Focusing in this way is healing to the body. Practicing these techniques has been shown to decrease stress disorders significantly.

Designing a Relaxation Program

Individualize the Program to the Patient

When you design a relaxation program for a patient, tailor the program to that patient's traits. Some factors to consider are the patient's attention span, receptivity, and ability to become absorbed in relaxation techniques. The ideal patient for relaxation techniques has a long attention span, is responsive and open to the techniques, and is able to become deeply absorbed in them. This patient can benefit from a long, deeply relaxing program. At the other end of the spectrum, some patients become fidgety immediately and their attention wanders. These patients need a quicker, more instant approach.

Try to use your patient's particular talents and skills. Some patients are adept at imaging; others are less able to image visually but are highly sensitive to sounds or to touch. In the case of an image of light, for example, some patients primarily "see" the light, some patients primarily "hear" it (as a buzzing), and others primarily "feel" it as warmth. Explore which sensory modality your patient uses most. You can then emphasize that modality in your imagery.

Aim toward capturing the patient's experience as fully as possible rather than suggesting ideas of your own. This will help you design a program that is a good fit for your patient.

Stylistic Concerns

Everything in your style should aim toward soothing and relaxing the patient. Speak softly, slowly, clearly, repetitively, rhythmically. Aim toward being easy to listen to, easy to hear. Maintain a steady flow. Keep paraphrasing. Use long, wordy, ambling sentences. Speak in a pleasant, lilting tone, in a voice similar to one you might use to put a child to sleep.

Always phrase your suggestions in a positive way: for example, say, "You will become more relaxed," rather than "You will become less tense" or "You will not tense." Use words that are positive, rather than negative or discordant: for example, say, "The birds sing in the sky" rather than "The birds cry in the sky," because "cry" suggests negative affect. Be light, uplifting, comforting.

Avoid stimulating the patient in any way. Do not be overly dramatic or speak so low that the patient must strain to hear. Avoid using any words the patient associates with stress. Avoid summoning material that is psychologically charged. Avoid surprising the patient in any way. Just say what the patient will hear as most soothing.

Help patients become comfortable. Have them sit back in a reclining chair or lie on the couch. Tell them to take off their glasses, remove their shoes, loosen their ties, and so on. Shut out outside sounds. Dim the lights. As much as possible, make sure you will not be disturbed.

Sample Relaxation Techniques

Here is a sample script for a relaxation session:

1. Progressive muscle relaxation of eight muscle groups
2. Deepening relaxation
3. A breathing meditation
4. Pleasant imagery
5. Healing imagery directed at the patient's stress symptoms
6. Alerting

Feel free to use this script, or make up your own with the patient. Just remember to aim consistently toward making the patient feel calm and relaxed.

We recommend that you tape the relaxation session and give the patient the tape to take home to use for practice.

Progressive Muscle Relaxation Training

Progressive muscle relaxation training (Jacobson 1938) is a good place to start. It can serve as a prelude to any of the other techniques. In progressive muscle relaxation training, we teach the patient to systematically tense and relax large muscle groups in the body. Common muscle groups used include upper arms, lower arms, upper legs, lower legs, abdomen, chest, shoulders, neck, and forehead.

The rationale is simple: A person cannot be tense and relaxed at the same time.

> *Therapist:* We want you to learn to notice when your body is tensing up, and to relax your body whenever it happens.
>
> With practice, you can learn to keep your body calm under stress. Not only will you deal with the stressor better, but also your physical stress symptoms will decrease.

We usually select at most eight muscle groups, based on discussion with the patient about his or her particular stress symptoms. If the patient has gastrointestinal problems, we include the abdomen as one of the muscle groups. If the person has headaches, we include the neck and forehead. In addition, we select muscle groups with a view toward conveying a sense of covering the whole body.

Give the patient a rationale for tension-relaxation exercises.

> *Therapist:* We have found that one good way to relax muscles is to tense them first. So for each muscle group, first we want you to tense the muscles and then we want you to relax them.

Go through the muscle groups, teaching the patient how to tense and relax each one. Here are some suggestions based upon Bernstein and Borkovec (1973). Have the patient tense each muscle group for about ten seconds. Then, instruct the patient to take a deep breath and, in time with the exhale, slowly relax the muscle group. As the patient exhales and relaxes the muscle group, the patient can think the word *relax*.

As you instruct the patient, write down the muscle groups you have chosen and the way to tense each one. Put this into the patient's Mastering Depression Notebook.

Make sure the patient is breathing correctly, slowly, and through the diaphragm. If the patient has trouble breathing correctly, then go through the breathing exercises presented in Managing Panic Attacks, below.

Tell patients to tense their muscles gently. It should not hurt to tense. In addition, tell patients that it is not necessary to do the exercise perfectly. In fact, the exercises can be done any number of ways; as long as they feel the muscle group tensing they are doing fine.

Lower arms	Put your arms straight out in front of you with palms down. Make two fists. Pull the fists toward you by bending your wrists.
Upper arms	Tense your upper arms by pulling your elbows down and at the same time as close to your body as you can without touching. Remember not to tense your lower arms—let your lower arms hang loosely.
Lower legs	Extend your legs straight in front of you. Pull your toes toward your body by bending your ankles.

Upper legs	Tense the front and back muscles in your upper legs, remembering to keep your lower legs relaxed.
Abdomen	Tense your abdomen as though a pillow were about to hit you in the stomach.
Chest	Take a deep breath and hold it, and at the same time pull your shoulders back and try to make your shoulder blades touch. Feel the tension like a ring circling around your chest and back.
Shoulders	Shrug your shoulders, bringing your shoulders up to your ears.
Neck	Press the back of your neck straight back against the chair.
Forehead	You can do this in two steps. First, tense your lower forehead by pulling your eyebrows together, then relax. Second, tense your upper forehead by raising your eyebrows, then relax.
Jaw	Gently bite your teeth together and pull the corners of your mouth back.

After you have selected the muscle groups and taught the patient how to tense and relax each one, you are ready to go through the procedure.

TENSING AND RELAXING EIGHT MUSCLE GROUPS

Therapist: (Turns on tape.) This is a relaxation session. Sit back on the couch and close your eyes. Let your body feel supported and comfortable. Empty your mind of everything but my voice. Let all other sounds around you fade away. Just listen to my voice and let yourself begin to relax.

We'll begin by tensing your lower arms. Focus on the feeling of tension in your lower arms. (Wait ten seconds.)

Now, take a deep breath and relax. (Pause until the patient has finished relaxing the muscles.) Focus on the feeling of relaxation in your lower arms. Notice how your lower arms feel different than when they were tense.

The relaxation is growing deeper and still deeper. You are relaxed, sleepy and relaxed. (Time with the patient's inhale.) With each breath you take in your relaxation increases; (time with the patient's exhale:) and each time you breathe out the relaxation gently radiates throughout your body. (Pause.)

Now, tense the muscles in your upper arms. Focus on the tension. (Wait ten seconds.)

Now, take a deep breath and relax. (Pause.) Focus on the feeling of relaxation in your upper arms. (Pause.)

You feel more and more relaxed, drowsy and relaxed. As you become more relaxed you feel yourself settling deep into the couch. Your body feels warm, heavy, comfortable, and relaxed.

Now, tense the muscles in your lower legs. Focus on the tension. (Wait ten seconds.)

Take a deep breath and relax. Focus on the feelings of relaxation in your lower legs. (Pause.) Notice how your lower legs feel different than when they were tense.

You are becoming more and more relaxed, peaceful and relaxed. As you become more relaxed, your breathing becomes slow and deep. You are peaceful. Your mind and your body are peaceful.

Now, tense the muscles in your upper legs. Focus on the tension in your upper legs. (Wait ten seconds.)

Take a deep breath and relax. (Pause.) Focus on the feelings of relaxation in your legs.

You are breathing slowly and deeply, slowly and deeply, as though you are falling asleep. You relax and you let your mind become calm. You relax and you let your body become calm. You feel pleasant and peaceful. (Pause.)

Now tense the muscles in your abdomen. Focus on the feeling of tension. (For the abdomen, wait ten seconds, and skip the part about taking a deep breath. It is too difficult to take a deep breath with one's abdomen tensed, and patients get confused. After ten seconds, say:) Now, relax. Focus on the feeling of relaxation in your stomach.

You are breathing slowly and deeply, slowly and deeply. You are becoming more and more deeply relaxed. Your body is peaceful, warm, and relaxed. (Pause.)

Now, tense the muscles in your chest. (As with the abdomen, wait ten seconds and skip taking a breath.) Now, relax. Focus on the feeling of relaxation in your chest.

You are becoming more and more relaxed, comfortable and relaxed. As you become more relaxed a feeling of well-being gently suffuses your mind and your body.

Now, tense the muscles in your shoulders. Focus on the feelings of tension. (Wait ten seconds.)

Now, take a deep breath and relax. Focus on the feeling of relaxation in your shoulders.

You are becoming more and more relaxed, drowsy and relaxed. As you become more relaxed, you are filled with a feeling of peace.

Now, tense the muscles in your neck, and focus on the feeling of tension. (Wait ten seconds.) Take a deep breath and relax. Focus on the feeling of relaxation. (Pause.)

Now I want you to relax all the muscles of your body: Just focus on your muscles, and let them become more and more deeply relaxed. Focus on your lower arms (pause); your upper arms (pause); your lower legs (pause); your upper legs (pause); your abdomen (pause); your chest (pause); your shoulders (pause); and your neck (pause). Just let yourself become more and more relaxed—warm, peaceful, comfortable, and relaxed. (Pause ten seconds.)

DEEPENING RELAXATION

Therapist: Now I am going to help you to achieve an even deeper state of relaxation. In a moment I will begin counting from one to five, and as I count, you will become more and more deeply relaxed.

(Try to time your counts to the patient's inhalations.) Ready, one (pause until end of inhale). You are becoming more and more deeply relaxed. Two (pause). More and more relaxed. Three (pause). Four (pause). More and more relaxed. Five (pause). You are deeply relaxed. (Pause ten seconds.)

A Breathing Meditation

Therapist: Now I'd like you to remain in your very relaxed state, and I'd like you to begin to focus just on your breathing. Breathe slowly and deeply, through your diaphragm. Notice the cool air as you breathe in (pair with inhalation), and the warm, moist air as you breathe out (pair with exhalation). Just continue to attend to your breathing, and each time you exhale, mentally repeat the word *relax.* Inhale (pair with inhalation), exhale (pair with exhalation), relax. . . . Inhale, exhale, relax. . . . Inhale, exhale, relax. . . . Inhale, exhale, relax. . . . Inhale, exhale, relax. (Pause ten seconds.)

Pleasant Imagery

You can use one of the scripts presented here, or you could have developed an individualized script beforehand in collaboration with the patient. The pleasant image can be drawn from the patient's actual experiences or it can be totally imaginary. The essential feature is that the patient respond to the image with a feeling of calm.

The more vivid the image is, the more effective it will be. Help the patient make the image vivid. If possible, include all of the five senses: sight, sound, touch, taste, smell. Remember to emphasize the patient's primary sensory modality. Try to capture every aspect of a peaceful moment in time.

Therapist: Now I want you to remain in your very relaxed state, and I want you to begin to imagine you are standing in a meadow filled with wildflowers. The flowers are yellow and purple. The sun is bright and warm, and a cool breeze brushes across your face. The flowers move gently in the wind.

You raise your eyes and see the mountains in the distance. The mountains are tall and strong and comforting. You breathe deeply and you draw strength from the mountains.

You close your eyes and raise your face to the warm, bright sun. You breathe slowly and deeply. The air is fragrant with the sweet smell of the wildflowers. You hear the sounds of birds singing in the sky. As the wind brushes your upturned face you feel a moment of total peace.

Here is another pleasant image, using what is perhaps the most popular one—the ocean.

Therapist: Now I want you to remain in your very relaxed state, and I want you to begin to imagine you are standing on the beach by the ocean. The sun is warm and bright. In front of you you see the white sand and the blue ocean, and the blue sky with white clouds floating. You watch the blue waves brushing gently against the shore.

You close your eyes and raise your face to the warm, bright sun. The sand feels cool and firm beneath your feet. You listen to the slow, rhythmic sound of the waves. A cool, slightly damp breeze brushes your face, and you smell the faint, sharp smell of salt in the wind. You hear the sound of the wind blowing gently in the distance, and the sound of gulls cawing in the sky.

As warm light bathes your face and gently radiates through your being, you know a moment of total peace.

HEALING IMAGERY DIRECTED AT THE
PATIENT'S STRESS SYMPTOMS

Tell patients to close their eyes and to visualize their stress symptom as an image. Help the patient make the image as vivid as possible. Then work together to construct an image of the stress symptom healing.

For example, a patient might visualize arthritis pain as fire in his joints. The fire is burning, hot, red. You and the patient could then construct an image of a cool, blue light emanating outward from the center of the patient's body, flowing through his joints, soothing and healing the red fire, gently turning it into cool blue, fading all the pain.

Here are some suggestions for some of the disorders. Feel free to use them, or, even better, work with patients to make up your own.

Asthma (or other breathing problems)
"Breathe slowly and deeply, with a slow, steady rhythm. Imagine the cool, fresh air moving in and out of your lungs; cool, fresh air passing smoothly through the branches in your lungs. Imagine the branches of your lungs opening, smoothing, clearing, the fresh, cool air rushing easily through. It is so easy to breathe, so easy."

Tension headaches
"Imagine your headache as a tight, cold, hard, dark ring around your head. Now imagine this ring gently warming, becoming soft, warm, loose, light. Imagine the ring becoming soft, warm, loose, and light. Soon the ring will be so light that it dissolves completely. The ring will be gone, and your head will feel relaxed and light."

Migraine headaches

"Imagine your headache as a throbbing red pulse inside your head. Now imagine a cool, white light bathing your head, bathing the red pulse, turning it pink, slowing it, soothing it. Imagine the pink fading to white and the throbbing becoming still. Imagine your headache cooling, fading, disappearing into the healing white light that suffuses your head and stills the throbbing, cools the burning, dissolves the pain, until all there is is cool, white light."

Insomnia

"Imagine a soft, warm, blue glow emanating from the center of your body and gently radiating outward from your center, soothing, comforting, relaxing. The warm, blue light surrounds you, holds you, comforts you. In the gentle glow of the blue light your body relaxes, your mind relaxes, and you feel peace . . . peace . . . peace. The soft, blue, warm light radiates from your center, and your body is so comfortable, your mind is so comfortable, and you feel peace . . . peace . . . peace." (End an insomnia tape here. Do not add the alerting, below.)

Gastrointestinal problems

"Focus on your abdomen and relax that area. Let all tension drain away. Imagine a warm, white light flowing through your intestines, soothing and relaxing, smoothing away all tension, cleansing, healing. Imagine your intestines bathed in the warm glow of this warm, white light, cleansing, healing, soothing, relaxing."

Panic attacks

"Imagine the panic is a frightened bird inside you, fluttering and scared. Now imagine a warm purple light coming from your heart, soothing, quieting, comforting the bird. Imagine that you whisper to the bird, 'You are safe. I will take care of you.' Your heart bathes the bird in the warm purple light, and the bird is happy, peaceful, quiet, and calm, gently rocking in the cradle of your body."

Chronic pain

"Focus on the area of your body that hurts you. Now imagine the pain as a hot red mass, pulsating in your body. Now imagine a cool, white light, flowing from a spot at the center of the area, draining away the red, draining away the heat, lightening, cooling, soothing, relaxing. As the cool, white light radiates through the area, imagine the red turning to pink (pause), and the pink fading into cool white."

AN ALERTING

The purpose of the alerting is to bring the patient back to a normal state of alertness, feeling relaxed, refreshed, and peaceful.

Therapist: Now I am going to help you to return to a normal state of alertness. In a moment I'll begin counting backward from five to one. As I count, you will become more and more alert, until, when I get to one, you will be entirely woken up to your normal state. You will feel alert, peaceful, and relaxed, as though you have just awakened from a refreshing nap.

Ready (pause), five. You feel more and more alert. Four (pause). You feel very refreshed. Three (pause). You are peaceful and relaxed. Two (pause). You feel very alert. You have a feeling of well-being. One (pause). Now you open your eyes and feel completely alert, peaceful, relaxed, and refreshed. (Pause twenty seconds.)

Ask the patient for feedback: "How was that?" Encourage the patient to describe the experience fully.

Dealing with Problems

Convey a spirit of openness and acceptance so that patients feel free to tell you about difficulties they are having following the program. Noncompliance with the program is an indirect sign that the patient is having difficulties. When this happens, treat the patient's noncompliance as a problem to be solved in treatment by the two of you working together. Deal with problems in a routine manner, with an air of confidence that the patient will eventually master the techniques and benefit from them. Try not to respond in a way that makes patients feel that their problems are unusual or strange. Assure them that their problems are common, solutions exist, and most likely the problems will disappear as they practice the relaxation program. This will help them feel relaxed and competent.

Keep asking for feedback. This is the best way to ensure that the program is appropriate. Reward the patient for feedback. Listen to it carefully, mirror it back to the patient, validate it. Incorporate it into subsequent sessions. Eliminate words or images the patient finds stressful; add positive ones the patient suggests. Lengthen or shorten the program, as the patient requests. Modulate your style in accord with the patient's responses.

While undergoing relaxation procedures, sometimes patients exhibit disruptive behaviors such as laughing, scratching, moving, speaking, opening their eyes. You can simply ignore most of these behaviors and they will gradually disappear. If a behavior persists, then instruct the patient to cease the behavior as part of the relaxation patter.

Patients may tell you they are having intrusive thoughts that distract them. Tell them that if their mind wanders, not to worry, but just to quietly bring their attention back to the relaxation procedure. Eventually they will learn to become more focused.

Homework Practice

Instruct patients about the importance of practice.

> *Therapist:* I want to spend some time talking about how you should practice your relaxation program if you want it to be maximally effective.
>
> Relaxation techniques can have a powerful effect on your life, but you will only get out of them what you put into them. The more you practice, the more skilled you will become at keeping your body and mind calm and centered as you go through your life, even in times of stress.
>
> I would like you to practice in two ways:

1. *Practice every day.* Do a relaxation practice every day.

   For the next few weeks, your daily relaxation practice should be listening to the tape and doing the procedures. Create a place where you can relax—you need a comfortable chair, couch, or bed, quiet, dim lighting, and an undisturbed period of time—and go there every day.

This should be your daily practice until you are highly skilled at becoming deeply relaxed in this way. Once you have become highly skilled, you can design other types of daily practices. At that time perhaps you will want to design relaxation practices in different locations, or during other activities, or in different bodily positions. But I want you to make a commitment that every day you will do one thing to practice your relaxation techniques.

2. *Practice every time you feel stressed.* The second way I want you to practice your relaxation techniques is to use them each time you feel stressed. Feeling stressed is a cue for you to use a relaxation technique.

How will you know that you are stressed? You will know from the situation (if it is obviously stressful: you are trying to get up the courage to ask someone to go on a date, for example, or you are late for work); or you will know from your body (you feel your muscles beginning to tense, or the first stirrings of your stress symptom).

If you watch, you will start to notice whenever you are stressed. This is your cue. Take a deep breath. Relax your muscles. Tell yourself to relax. Close your eyes for a moment and bring up your pleasant image. Remember that feeling of peace. As you handle the situation, keep your body relaxed and your breathing slow, deep, and regular. If you feel your stress symptom, use the image of your stress symptom healing.

Ask patients to regard each occurrence of stress as an opportunity to practice their relaxation skills.

IMPROVING PRODUCTIVITY

Very often depressed patients have "let things go" in whatever it is they call their work—their job, their schoolwork, taking care of their family, managing their domestic affairs, their hobbies. It may be that their productivity is chronically low due to poor work habits and psychological conflicts about work, and that all this contributed to the onset of their depression in the first place; or it may be that, because of their depression, they have lost the interest and motivation to keep doing their work at a satisfactory level.

Whether low productivity is a cause or result of their depression, very often depressed patients can benefit from cognitive-behavioral approaches to increasing productivity. They can learn ways to improve their work habits, and they can recognize and resolve psychological issues that are blocking them from reaching their full potential in their work lives.

Psychological Issues

There are three major reasons patients underachieve: anxiety, anger, and lack of self-discipline.

> Zack belongs to the first type. He writes for a travel magazine. Zack is fine when he is traveling and doing research, but when it is time to write an article he has a problem being productive. He procrastinates. He puts off starting to write until it is almost too late. And then, as the deadline looms, he does a mad rush at the end, staying up till all hours, and, drained and exhausted, gets it done just in time. Zack explains to us that he needs a deadline hanging over his head to get himself to work.

Zack's procrastination is due primarily to anxiety. He feels overwhelmed. Each article he has to write seems so *big*. He has performance anxiety—his mind is filled with negative thoughts about how people will judge his work. The voice of his "inner critic" intrudes constantly through his automatic thoughts. He feels that he has to do the task perfectly. Anything less than perfection represents complete failure. Each time he thinks about working he feels anxious and prefers to avoid it.

Of course, the problem with avoidance as a coping strategy is that it just makes things worse. The longer Zack puts off starting, the more overwhelmed he feels. As the deadline looms closer his anxiety intensifies. This is the neurotic paradox of avoidance: in the moment Zack avoids he feels relief, but in the long run he feels even more anxious.

Mara belongs to the second type. She procrastinates because she is angry. Procrastination is a way for her to express her anger. Mara and her husband, Brian, own and manage a clothing store. Even though they are partners, she feels that he treats her as though he were the boss and she the employee. Whenever he tells her to do something she resents it. But rather than expressing her anger openly to her husband, she expresses it passive-aggressively, by silently resisting. When Brian asks her for the work, she makes excuses. Hence, she is chronically behind in her work, and the success of the store suffers as a result.

Passive-aggressive behaviors such as agreeing to do something and not following through are indirect ways of expressing anger. They irritate other people, but it is difficult for other people to know whether the passive-aggressive person intends the irritation. Brian gets frustrated with Mara, but he does not know for sure that she is angry. In fact, Mara herself is only dimly aware of her anger. It is also worth noting that in the way she is expressing her anger, Mara is hurting herself as much as she is hurting Brian.

Sylvia belongs to the third type. She lacks self-discipline. As a child she was the only child of wealthy parents, and she was spoiled and indulged. Her parents gave her everything, did everything for her. She never had to develop self-discipline and build skills. Now Sylvia is trying to get ahead in the music business. She would eventually like to become a producer. Although she is smart and sociable, in the ten years she has worked at her company, she has been promoted only once. Thus far she is an underachiever.

Sylvia expects others to compensate for her lack of discipline and feels annoyed when they refuse. Instead of working on developing the discipline and the skills she lacks, she blames others for her failures at work. Consequently, she has alienated her colleagues and displeased her bosses, as well as failing to produce high-quality work.

Conceptualize the Problem

The first thing you must do is to conceptualize the problem. Most likely your patient will fall into one (or more) of the three types we have described. What are the psychological issues that block full productivity for your patient?

When anxiety is the cause of low productivity, anxiety-reducing techniques can be helpful. Patients can do some form of relaxation technique before starting work. They can monitor their negative thoughts and evaluate them more objectively. Where their thoughts are irrational, they can replace them with more realistic and constructive thoughts. They can break the task into smaller steps and learn to tolerate anxiety gradually (see the behavioral treatment material on managing anxiety).

When anger is the culprit, help the patient become more assertive (see Assertiveness Training, above). Whether the patient is too passive or too aggressive (or swings back and forth between the two), assertiveness training can help the patient acknowledge and express anger in more positive ways.

When patients lack self-discipline, the procedures we describe in Work Habits, below, might be helpful. Before turning to them, make a list with patients of the negative consequences of their poor self-discipline. They can read the list whenever they need to build motivation to work.

Work Habits: Stimulus Control, Goal Setting, Time Management, and Self-Reinforcement

Present patients with a rationale for improving their work habits.

> *Therapist:* As we've discussed, one thing that contributes to your depression is the trouble you're having getting things done. You're not producing the amount or quality of work that others expect from you and that you want from yourself.
>
> Let's talk about your work habits. Let's talk about changes you might make that will enable you to be more productive. This way you can ease back into working productively now, and be less likely to get depressed in the future. The more you fulfill your

true potential in your work, the happier and less depressed you will be.

The techniques we are going to talk about have considerable research support. Almost anyone can become more productive by using them.

Present patients with the following techniques derived from cognitive-behavioral principles.

Stimulus Control

Instruct patients to create a place where they work and only work. This is especially important for patients who work at home or in chaotic environments and need a boundary between their work and non-work worlds.

Everything patients see and hear in their workplace should promote a focus on work. It should be quiet, organized, comfortable, well lit, and undisturbed. There should be nothing distracting, nothing unpredictable.

Help patients plan the design of their work space. Give the assembling of this space as a homework assignment.

Goal Setting

Patients should do an overview of their current work goals. You can do it with them. Help them prioritize. Together select an appropriate project to serve as the goal you will work toward completing in therapy. Make sure this project is clearly defined and manageable.

Together list all the steps the patient has to take to complete this project. Focus on one of these steps as a place to begin. Ask the patient to commit to working on this step each day during the following week (you can exclude the weekend if you wish).

Instruct patients as follows: At the beginning of each work session, they should set a goal for the day. The goal should be product oriented, rather than time oriented (i.e., one page of writing rather than one hour of writing). It is important that they start with a goal that is much smaller than the amount they eventually need or want to produce each day.

> *Therapist:* The key is to select a goal you know you can meet. If you are not sure that you can meet the goal, then it is too big. Tomorrow, when you sit down to write, what would be a goal for the day that you know you can meet?
>
> *Patient:* Well, I have to write at least five pages a day to meet my deadline with the publisher. I have to write at least that every day, if not more.
>
> *Therapist:* Right now I want you to ask yourself honestly, do you know for sure you can sit down tomorrow and write five pages? Is there any doubt in your mind?
>
> *Patient:* Of course. In fact, I know that there's no way I can do it. There's no way I can write five pages tomorrow.
>
> *Therapist:* Could you write one paragraph?
>
> *Patient:* Could I write one paragraph? Yes. I could. But I have to write much more than that.
>
> *Therapist:* I want you to trust me, trust that you will write more eventually. But tomorrow I want your goal to be to write one paragraph. I want this to be your goal each day next week: writing one paragraph per day.

Instruct patients to do no less and no more than their goal. When they have met their goal, they are finished working on the project for the day.

When patients have met their goal successfully for many days, they may gradually increase the goal for the day until they have reached a satisfactory level of productivity to complete the project. But they must always remember to keep the goal manageable.

If patients fail to meet their goal for the day, they are not permitted to increase the goal for the next day to make up for it. Rather, they must either keep the goal the same or decrease it. They are permitted to increase the goal only after meeting it successfully for several days.

For the first few weeks help patients set their daily goals; later they can set goals on their own and report to you. Tell patients that they will be more productive in the long run by setting small, reasonable goals each day and working steadily day after day.

> *Therapist:* Research shows that those who wait until they are inspired to work and then work in binges are less productive than those who practice discipline and work in the slow-and-steady fashion we have suggested. In fact, if you adopt this approach, you will find that inspiration happens more often. The quality as well as the quantity of your work will improve.

Time Management

As much as possible each day, patients should do their work on the project before any other activities. Once they have reached their goal for the day, they are finished, and can do whatever they like for the rest of the day. However, they cannot do any other (nonessential) activities or go to sleep that night until they have met their goal.

Ideally, patients would get up in the morning, wash, get dressed, eat breakfast, and then sit down to work. They would work steadily until they have reached their goal, perhaps breaking for lunch, then have the rest of the day free. However, if patients procrastinate, they might spend the whole day and night not working, and never have free time for other activities.

Self Reinforcement

Patients should reward themselves for reaching their goal for the day.

> *Therapist:* Rewarding yourself is a way of acknowledging what you have done. In fact, that is the most important reward you can give yourself—taking a moment to stop and acknowledge yourself for reaching a goal.
>
> The free time you have after reaching your goal for the day is another way you can reward yourself. Let's think of some other ways you can reward yourself for reaching your goal for the day.

Help patients develop a list of ways to reward themselves. Tell them to reward themselves each time they meet their goal for the day.

The rewards should be activities that are pleasant and self-nurturing: taking a walk, calling a friend, going out for coffee, getting a massage, swimming, going for a bicycle ride, playing a game, reading a novel, listening to music, buying oneself a gift. The rewards vary from patient to patient. Explore with patients what is most rewarding to them.

If it feels comfortable for you, you can tell patients they may leave a message on your answering machine when they have completed their goal for the day. This can serve as a reward as well.

MANAGING PANIC ATTACKS

Panic attacks are often an associated feature of depression. Since they can be extremely debilitating, it is important to help patients who have panic attacks learn to manage them. The cognitive-behavioral approach toward treating panic, like the cognitive-behavioral approach toward treating depression, is one of active coping.

Barlow (Barlow and Craske 1989) has developed an effective panic treatment. The treatment we present is based upon his approach, and includes the following components:

1. Education about panic attacks
2. Learning and practicing skills to control cognitive panic symptoms
3. Learning and practicing skills to control somatic panic symptoms
4. Gradual exposure to all feared symptoms and situations
5. Consideration of general stressors

Education about Panic Attacks

Give patients the Education about Panic Attacks handout (see Appendix I) to add to their notebook. Review it together. Discuss how the material relates to the patient's own experience. Answer any questions the patient might have.

Therapist: As defined in the 1994 *Diagnostic and Statistical Manual of Mental Disorders*, a panic attack is a sudden rush of intense fear—a feeling that something catastrophic is about to happen—accompanied by at least some of the following symptoms:

difficulty breathing
heart racing or pounding
pain or tightness in your chest
dizziness or light-headedness
trembling
numbness or tingling sensations
feeling of unreality
tightness or choking feeling in your throat
gastrointestinal disturbance
sweating
hot flashes or chills
fear of dying, going crazy, or losing control

Some people fear dying during panic attacks. They are afraid they will smother or have a heart attack, or that they have some terrible disease. Some people fear going crazy or losing control. They fear that they are having a nervous breakdown or that they will mentally drift into unreality and never return to a normal state again. They fear that they will fall, scream, run, cry, get sick, pass out. They are afraid that they will lose control and jump from a height or swerve into traffic with their car. Or they fear becoming nonfunctional.

What you fear during a panic attack depends largely on which symptoms you feel and focus on most. Some people focus on the heart symptoms and fear they are having a heart attack. Others focus on the feeling of unreality and fear they are going crazy, or they focus on the dizziness and fear they are passing out, or they focus on the gastrointestinal symptoms and fear they are getting sick, or they focus on the breathing symptoms and fear they are smothering.

Agoraphobia Panickers often develop phobias of specific places or things. Some phobias you might have include being alone, being in the middle of crowds (at theaters, stores, concerts, etc.), riding forms of transportation (buses, trains, planes, cars, elevators, ski lifts), tunnels, bridges, heights, restaurants, traffic jams, taking medication (gas at the dentist, anesthesia, prescription medications), going far from home, going out of the reach of medical help, certain kinds of physical exertion (exercise, sex, amusement park rides), various foods, and waiting in line. If you have panic disorder and you have some of these phobias, then we say that you are agoraphobic.

Agoraphobics are different than other kinds of phobics. Other phobics fear a specific danger in the world. They fear dogs, cats, spiders, snakes, airplane crashes. They can simply avoid the thing that they fear and feel relatively safe. But not agoraphobics. The danger agoraphobics fear comes from within, from their own body, their own mind, in the form of these panic symptoms that seem to come out of nowhere and race out of control.

Other phobics fear things in the world that they believe are dangerous. They fear animals because animals can bite; they fear airplanes because airplanes can crash; they fear germs because germs can cause sickness. However, when an agoraphobic really explores what he or she is afraid of, it is always the panic attack itself, not the danger inherent in the situation.

For example, if you are agoraphobic, you do not fear airplanes because they can crash; you fear them because you might have a panic attack in the plane and be trapped there. It is the panic symptoms, not crashing, that you fear. You believe that the symptoms are dangerous. It is the symptoms that convince you that you are about to die, go crazy, or lose control. Ultimately what you fear is the panic itself. You fear the fear.

Agoraphobics avoid going places where they might have a panic attack and be unable to get out or get help. These are their two main concerns. They need to know that they can get out of a place, and they need to know that they can get help if they need it. The places they fear most are those that trap them and those that cut them off from help.

Anticipatory anxiety When you have to go somewhere you become very anxious. You may worry for days. You think: What if I have a panic attack there? Will I be trapped? How embarrassing will it be for me to leave? Will I be able to get help? Will I be able to get home? Will I be alone?

This anticipatory anxiety is a feature of panic disorder, and it can be excruciating. Between attacks you live in dread of the next one, and, although you can guess, you can never be sure where or when the next one is going to strike. You might have safe people or safe places that make you feel better, but you cannot reach a feeling of total safety.

You can master your panic We always tell our panic-disorder patients that it is not the panic we are going to treat, but rather their reaction to the panic. They are going to learn to master the panic. The key to mastering panic attacks is to stop running away from them and start facing them and learning to control them. That this can be done we have witnessed hundreds of times. In your treatment you will learn how to master your panic attacks.

Teach patients about the fight-or-flight response.

> *Therapist:* Suppose you are walking into a store and as you open the door you see a man take out a gun and point it at the cashier's head. In the split second it takes you to understand what is happening, your body begins to react. Nature has prepared your body to react to such emergencies in some very helpful ways.
>
> You get a rush of adrenaline, which energizes you. Your senses suddenly all become more acute. You start to hyperventilate—your body takes in more oxygen, making more available for organs and muscles. Your heart pumps harder and faster, carrying the oxygen throughout your body. Unnecessary systems such as digestion shut down, preserving all your energy for the emergency at hand.
>
> This fight-or-flight response could save your life in this situation. If you were to run, you could run faster than normal. If you were to fight, you would be stronger and fight better than usual. Your body would perform at its peak.
>
> Let's suppose that you decide to run. As you turn you see another robber behind you, looking right at you, holding a gun. You are trapped.
>
> Nature has prepared you for this situation, too, with another response—the freeze response. It is the

opposite of fight-or-flight. Everything in your body slows down. You stop moving (probably a good idea when someone is pointing a gun at you), and may even feel frozen. Things seem unreal, dreamlike (which can be a blessing when reality is so bad). Your blood pressure drops (which makes you somewhat dizzy, but would help if you were shot because you would bleed a little less).

If you have panic disorder, the fight-or-flight or freeze response is what is happening to your body when you have a panic attack.

Teach patients the three laws of anxiety:

1. Panic is not dangerous.
2. Panic always ends.
3. Exposure decreases anxiety, and avoidance increases anxiety.

Therapist: There are three laws of anxiety that we would like to teach you. The first one is: Panic attacks are not dangerous. The fight-or-flight and freeze responses do not hurt you in any way. In the vast literature on panic, there is not a single reported case of someone dying, going crazy, or losing control during an attack. Afterward perhaps you are tired, but you have not been harmed.

Second, the panic always passes. Time alone ends a panic attack. The panic always comes to an end, and you always return to your normal state.

In fact, panic attacks are by their nature very quick. On their own they end in minutes. If they last longer, you are doing something to maintain them. What you are doing to maintain them has to do with the way you are thinking about the attacks; you are interpreting them as far more dangerous than they really are.

Third, exposure to the symptoms and situations that you fear decreases panic, and avoidance of the symptoms and situations maintains panic.

In fact, it is roughly true that, however anxious you are when you leave a situation, that's about how anxious you will be the next time you enter the situation.

For example, say you have a fear of riding the train. You get on the train, have a major panic attack, and flee at the height of anxiety at a station before your station—say, when you are at an 80 on a 0 to 100 anxiety scale. The next time you get on the train your anxiety will be 80, the same level as when you left the train before.

Now, say you stay on the train. Even if you do nothing to control your anxiety, eventually it will come down, because time alone always ends a panic attack. If you stayed on the train until your anxiety came down, say below 20 on a 0 to 100 anxiety scale, then the next time you got on the train your anxiety would be about a 20. Whatever level you are at when you leave the situation, that is about what level you will be at the next time you enter it. (One exception is if you wait a very long time before getting on the train again. If you avoid the train for a long period afterward, the anxiety will creep back up.)

Learning and Practicing Skills to
Control Cognitive Panic Symptoms

Discuss the central role of catastrophizing in maintaining panic symptoms.

> *Therapist:* Catastrophic thinking drives your panic attacks. Catastrophizing is jumping to the worst possible conclusion, without the evidence to warrant such a jump. The nickname for catastrophizing is "what if-ing": "What if I am having a heart attack?" "What if the panic never ends?" "What if I am having a nervous breakdown?" "What if I lose control and jump from this height?" "What if I smother to death?" "What if I fall and horribly embarrass myself?"
>
> As long as you continue to think catastrophically, you pour fuel on the fire of your panic attacks. Your catastrophic thoughts increase your physical symptoms, which in turn increase your catastrophic thoughts, in a vicious circle that can keep panic going for hours.
>
> Instead, think more realistically. Stop thinking that you are that one special person who will really die, go crazy, or lose control during a panic. Every panicker feels this way. Instead of telling yourself lies that scare you, tell yourself the truth.

Ask patients to make a commitment to filling out a Thought Record whenever they have panic attacks, even mild ones, paying special attention to identifying catastrophic, "what if" automatic thoughts, and decatastrophizing in the Rational Response column.

Make a flash card with the patient. A flash card can be a cue for patients to use their coping strategies. Patients can carry it with them and read it whenever they have panic symptoms.

Here is a blueprint. Tailor it to fit your patient's particular symptoms.

A Panic Attack Flashcard

Right now I am having panic symptoms. I am afraid that I am going to have a major attack and die, go crazy, or lose control.

However, I am catastrophizing. In reality no one has ever died, gone crazy, or lost control during a panic attack. In fact, I am experiencing the fight-or-flight or freeze response that is common to all living creatures who feel themselves threatened.

If I relax and do my breathing, the panic will pass and I will be my normal self again. The panic cannot harm me. I just have to stay in the situation and let it pass, and then it will be gone.

I can and will stay in the situation until the anxiety is gone. I will use my cognitive and somatic coping strategies. In this way I will gain mastery over my panic attacks.

Learning and Practicing Skills to Control Somatic Panic Symptoms

Here is a simple relaxation technique you can teach your patients. It has two parts: breathing and meditation. As you teach it to patients, write down simple directions to place in their Mastering Depression Notebook.

Demonstrate the breathing part. If you like, you can place one hand over your diaphragm (right above your navel), and the other on your chest. Tell patients that, when they are breathing correctly, only the bottom hand moves.

> *Therapist:* Breathe slowly and deeply. Try to take no more than eight to twelve breaths per minute. When you breathe, only your diaphragm should move. Your chest should be totally still.

Breathing this way will stop patients from hyperventilating, a major cause of panic symptoms.

Explain the meditation part of the exercise:

> *Therapist:* The meditation part follows the rhythm of your breathing. As you breathe in, slowly count, "one." As you breathe out, think the word *relax*. Then as you breathe in, think the word *two*. As you breathe out, think the word *relax*.
>
> (Demonstrates.) Three . . . relax. . . . Four . . . relax. . . . Five . . . relax. . . . Six . . . relax. . . . Go all the way up to ten. Just keep counting and repeating the word *relax* slowly in time to your breaths. Meditating this way can help center your body and your mind.

Instruct patients to practice the relaxation technique as a continuing homework assignment:

> *Therapist:* Practice this technique often. As you go about your day, notice your breathing. If you are breathing incorrectly (breathing too fast, breathing from your chest), correct your breathing. Learn to be mindful of your breathing.
>
> Research shows that many panickers chronically breathe incorrectly, even when they are not anxious. In fact, this habit of breathing incorrectly is probably

one major reason you have the attacks in the first place. Incorrect breathing sets up a physical vulnerability that stress then attacks.

In addition, use this technique whenever you feel anxious or have an attack. If you practice the technique and become skilled at it, using it can help immeasurably.

Gradual Exposure to All Feared Symptoms and Situations

This, ultimately, is the most important part of the treatment. Patients have to enter the situations they fear and practice managing their panic symptoms.

Make a Hierarchy

Working together with patients, make a hierarchy of symptoms and situations, using the usual 0 to 100 scale. Place a copy of the hierarchy in the patient's Mastering Depression Notebook.

0	25	50	75	100
No anxiety	Mild anxiety	Moderate anxiety	Extreme anxiety	As much anxiety as possible

Therapist: Let's make a list together of all the symptoms and situations you fear, ranging from situations that make you only mildly anxious all the way to the situations that you fear most.

Let's start with 25, mild anxiety. What is a situation or a symptom that makes you mildly anxious?

Here is a sample hierarchy for a 42-year-old agoraphobic patient named Leonard. Leonard is presented in the educational handout on panic you gave the patient (see Appendix I).

Level of anxiety	Situation
20:	Riding the elevator at work
25:	Working out at the gym
30:	Getting stuck in traffic on a side road
35:	Drinking caffeinated coffee
40:	Swimming underwater
45:	Being alone in my house during the day
50:	Riding the train to work
55:	Riding the ferry
60:	Watching movies about submarines, spaceships, airplanes, prison, people getting trapped or marooned
65:	Riding on the highway, little traffic
70:	Waking up in the middle of the day from a nap
80:	Getting anesthetic at the dentist
85:	Being alone in the house at night
90:	Going camping
100:	Riding on the highway in a lot of traffic
100:	Going on an airplane

Pick the easiest item and start with that. Instruct the patient to enter the situation for homework.

> *Therapist:* Now here is what you must remember. You have to stay in the situation until your anxiety comes down. If you flee from the situation at the height of your anxiety, the exposure will not help you.
>
> Use your cognitive and somatic coping skills to manage your anxiety as you stay in the situation.

For example, for his first item Leonard picked "riding the elevator." As a homework assignment between sessions, he got into an elevator, and his anxiety rose to a moderate level. He began practicing his breathing exercise and correcting his catastrophic thinking. Leonard rode the elevator up and down until his anxiety went away, that is, below 10 on the 0 to 100 anxiety scale.

Leonard practiced riding elevators until the situation no longer produced anxiety. He thus mastered the situation and was not afraid of it anymore. He then moved up to a slightly more difficult item.

Make sure you assign items for homework that are easy enough for patients to complete successfully. You should feel totally confident that the patient can master anxiety at this level. Work your way up the hierarchy slowly. It is better to choose an item that is too easy than one that is too hard.

Each time patients complete an exposure exercise, teach them to take a moment to acknowledge themselves. Patients often belittle the idea that they deserve praise for completing an exposure exercise. As Leonard said after completing his first exposure, "Big deal. Anyone can ride the elevator." Try to counter this tendency by pointing out to patients that each completed exposure is a step toward mastering their panic disorder.

Consideration of General Stressors

Discuss the relationship between panic attacks and stress.

Therapist: Panic disorder is a stress disorder. The symptoms flare up in times of stress and abate in times of calm. Like other stress disorders—migraine headaches, irritable bowel, skin rashes—your panic attacks are telling you something about your life. You need to listen to what they are telling you.

What are the stressors in your life, and how can you manage them better? How can you add activities that are more deeply fulfilling?

For some patients, panic attacks are secondary to another problem. For example, they occur because patients cannot manage their time well, or control their worries, or assert themselves in various situations. The consequences of the other problem throw these patients into a chronic state of anxiety, setting a platform for panic. In these cases, it is best to treat the primary problem. Utilizing the skills presented in the relevant chapters of this book will help these patients prevent the occurrence of their panic attacks.

MANAGING WORRY

Depressed patients often experience a significant amount of anxiety related to excessive worrying. Research shows that as many as one in four depressed patients also meet the diagnosis for generalized anxiety disorder. Teaching skills for managing worry is thus an important treatment component for many depressed patients.

Education about Anxiety and Worrying

Begin by educating the patient about the symptoms of worrying. Give the patient the handout Managing Worry (see Appendix I), and cover the material it presents.

> *Therapist:* Nearly everyone is familiar with worrying. We define worry as a chain of negative thoughts related to fears about the future. Typically, when you worry, you experience concern that something you desire might not happen, for example, you might get turned down for a raise, or something terrible might occur, for example, you might lose your job.
>
> A typical chain of worried thoughts might sound like this: "What if I can't meet my deadline for this project at work? My boss will be mad at me. I might get fired! How will I make the payments on the house? I won't be able to buy a new car, and the old one needs work. I'll have to spend money on the car instead of saving for the kids' education."
>
> Worry can be useful when it is productive, that is, when you use worrying as a cue to solve problems and prepare for future events. For example, a productive way to handle worrying about an exam is

by studying. If worrying motivates you to study, then it's a good thing. But worry becomes a problem when it is unproductive, or even destructive. Rather than solving problems, chronic worriers often just generate more and more worries.

Worrying can become a significant problem. Since it is often accompanied by a mixture of negative emotions, such as fear and apprehension, and physical sensations, such as muscle tension, heart palpitations, and upset stomach, worrying can have a large impact on how you feel both emotionally and physically. Worrying can lead to impaired functioning: for example, worrying can distract you from your work or rob you of your enjoyment of good things that are happening in your life. Certainly worrying can worsen your depression.

We know from research that, for the most part, people who are worriers do not have more stressful situations in their lives than people who are not worriers. Instead, whether or not you become a worrier seems to be a function of the way you think: worriers tend to see things as being more threatening than do nonworriers. In addition, worriers tend to feel they have less control over things that happen in their lives. It is possible that this negative view of the world as more threatening and less controllable was passed down to you by your parents.

Worriers typically focus on the worst possible features of any situation. As a result, they often feel as though a lot of negative things are happening, even though their worry is excessive and unrealistic.

Techniques for Managing Worry

Cognitive Techniques

Present the rationale for the use of cognitive techniques.

> *Therapist:* What most people naturally do to deal with worrying is try to distract themselves. However, this only works for a little while, and you soon find yourself wrapped up in the worries again. Distracting yourself from your worries doesn't solve them. To overcome your worries, you must confront them.
>
> As is the case with correcting other distorted negative emotions, the best way to deal with your worries is to focus on them and learn to analyze the accuracy of your thinking. Often, the thoughts associated with worry are exaggerated or unrealistic, and you are thus worrying unnecessarily. If you could train yourself to be more realistic, you might find that many of your worries are not as serious as you originally thought.
>
> Here are three simple steps from a cognitive therapy technique called logical analysis that you can use to reduce your worry. The steps are in the handout that I just gave you to put in your depression notebook.

1. *Write down the thoughts that are going through your mind as you are worrying.* This will teach you to become aware of your thinking.

   Be as specific as possible. Try to identify the exact prediction you are making about the future. For example, don't write: "I'm worrying about work"; write:

"If I miss the deadline on this work project I will lose my job."

2. *Examine how realistic your thoughts are.* Use your cognitive techniques to evaluate whether your thoughts are distorted or inaccurate. Are you thinking logically? Examine the evidence: Do you have evidence that supports or refutes your thoughts? Are you accounting for all the aspects of the situation or only the negative ones?

    Again, be specific: for example, "Have I missed deadlines before? Have others missed deadlines? What usually happens?"

    You can fill out a Thought Record or The Steps to Constructing a Rational Response form to help you with this step (see Appendix I).

3. *Now come up with a new thought—a rational response— that is more realistic than the original thought.* For example, "Missing the deadline on this project is not something I want to happen, but it is very unlikely that I will lose my job because of this one event, even if my boss is angry."

Another strategy you can teach patients is decatastrophizing. Worriers tend to catastrophize; they constantly ask themselves, "What if the worst possible thing that can happen does happen?" Worriers can turn almost any situation into a potential catastrophe; one minor worry can snowball into several major worries. For example, following a minor quarrel with her boyfriend, a young woman might worry that he will break up with her and then she will be alone forever.

Worriers often become stuck in the "what if." They ask themselves what if the worst possible thing happens, and then worry about it endlessly, without ever actually pushing through the what if and asking themselves, "What would actually happen if the worst thing actually happened?" This is called decatastrophizing, or pushing through the what if. For example, the therapist might say to the female patient who is worrying about losing her boyfriend: "Well, what if he did break up with you? What would happen then?" Through directed questioning, the therapist would guide the patient to see that she could survive a breakup and go on with her life.

> *Therapist:* Instead of repetitively worrying, "What if the worst thing happens," or catastrophizing, I want you to decatastrophize. This means to ask yourself: "Well, what if the worst thing happened? What would happen then? How would I cope with it?" Imagine the worst possible thing happening and everything that would result from it, and how you would want to deal with it. Having solutions will give you more of a sense of control over the situation and will help you to feel less helpless.

Present Behavioral Techniques

The main behavioral technique is stimulus control.

> *Therapist:* Stimulus control comes from the learning-theory branch of psychology. We know that when people do something in one situation, they are likely to do it again the next time they are in that situation. Because you can worry nearly any time and any place, your worrying has become associated with many situations. So, to reduce the frequency of your worrying,

one way is to limit when and where your worrying occurs.

For example, you could decide to set a thirty-minute "worry period," to take place at the same time and at the same place each day. For that thirty-minute period, you would try to spend the entire time worrying. If you want, you could close your eyes and think in detail about all the things you are worried about, or you could write out your worries, or you could speak to other people about them. You could do whatever you want to try to fill the entire thirty-minute period with worrying.

But, every time you start to worry at any other time or any other place, you must stop and instruct yourself to postpone your worrying until your next worry period. If you want to make sure you don't forget the worry, then you could write it down.

You will have to learn to identify when you are starting to worry. Self-monitoring your worrying will help you to do this.

To stop worrying during nonworry times, replace worried thoughts by distracting yourself with something else, like listening to music or taking a walk outside. Every time the worry comes back, notice it and then distract yourself, until eventually you let the worry go.

Patients can use self-reinforcement for successfully postponing worry. Help patients compose a list of ways they could reward themselves whenever they are able to use the technique to postpone worrying, and place a copy of the list in their Mastering Depression Notebook.

CONCLUDING REMARKS

As a cognitive-behavioral therapist treating depression, your goal is to ally with the patient against the depression. The depression is not the patient. The depression is the enemy within the patient; it is the invader you and the patient are trying to drive out. Remembering this will help you cope positively with the patient's resistance to change. When the patient expresses feelings of worthlessness and hopelessness, it is not the patient's voice but the voice of the depression that you are hearing. Join with the healthy part of the patient in fighting this voice.

Overcoming depression with cognitive-behavioral therapy requires a commitment to reason and self-discipline. Both the therapist and patient must make this commitment. Each time the patient's depression exerts an effect, the therapist and patient have the opportunity to practice fighting the depression using somatic, cognitive, emotional, and behavioral self-control techniques.

APPENDIX I: HANDOUTS

SAMPLE ITEMS FROM THE BECK DEPRESSION INVENTORY (BDI)

0 I am not particularly discouraged about the future.
1 I feel discouraged about the future.
2 I feel I have nothing to look forward to.
3 I feel that the future is hopeless and that things cannot improve.

0 I get as much satisfaction out of things as I used to.
1 I don't enjoy things the way I used to.
2 I don't get real satisfaction out of anything anymore.
3 I am dissatisfied or bored with everything.

The BDI contains 21 items. The Psychological Corporation has granted us permission to reprint two items to provide an example of the type of items on the inventory. To purchase a full version of the BDI, contact the Psychological Corporation, 555 Academic Court, San Antonio, TX 78204. Telephone: 1-800-228-0752.

EDUCATION ABOUT DEPRESSION

What Is Depression?

According to the 1994 *Diagnostic and Statistical Manual of Mental Disorders* (*DSM-IV*), the book that professionals use to diagnose emotional problems, the symptoms of depression are as follows. If you are depressed, you probably have most (but not necessarily all) of these symptoms.

1. *Feeling depressed* Most of the time you feel down, sad, empty, discouraged. You may cry a lot, or you may feel like crying but be unable to cry. Feeling irritable is also common.

2. *Loss of interest* You have a loss of interest and pleasure in life so that you have to push yourself to do things you used to enjoy. This often includes a loss of interest in sex. It becomes difficult for you to anticipate that anything might be pleasurable.

3. *Change in appetite for food* The most usual picture is that you lose your appetite. Food doesn't interest you. You have to push yourself to eat, and you may lose weight.

Sometimes people eat more when they are depressed. They use food as a source of comfort or as a way to fill a sense of emptiness. If this is true of you, you may gain rather than lose weight.

4. *Disturbed sleep* You sleep much less or much more than normal. If you are sleeping less, perhaps you can't fall asleep, or you keep waking up during the night, or you wake up too early and can't go back to sleep.

If you are sleeping too much, you may be taking long naps during the day or sleeping longer during the night.

5. *Feeling agitated or slowed down* Your body, your mind, and your speech are either going too fast or too slow. Either you are agitated and restless or you are sluggish.

6. *Loss of energy* You feel tired, drained. Even small tasks seem exhausting. In extreme cases, you find it hard to do the normal activities of everyday life, such as showering, dressing, shopping, and preparing meals.

7. *Feelings of worthlessness or guilt* Your self-esteem is low. You may feel worthless or bad, and even hate yourself. You may believe that your depression is a punishment you deserve.

You are probably angry at yourself about the depression as well—about how much you let the depression interfere with your personal and work life.

8. *Difficulty thinking* You can't think as well as you can normally. You have trouble concentrating and making decisions.

9. *Thoughts about suicide* Most likely you feel hopeless. You may have thoughts that life is not worth living or you would rather be dead. You may believe that others would be better off without you.

You may fantasize about committing suicide, and may actually develop a plan for where, when, and how you might do it.

It is important that you share with your therapist all your thoughts about suicide. If at any point during treatment you feel that you might attempt suicide or any form of self-harm, contact your therapist immediately. If you cannot reach your therapist, contact the doctor on call for your therapist.

Depression may occur in one or more intense episodes (major depression), or it may underlie your life at a less intense level most of the time for years (dysthymia). Twice as many women have depressive episodes as men. However, girl children and boy children are equally likely to have depressive episodes. Depression tends to run in families. However, rates of depression are not related to ethnic group, level of education, income, or marital status.

Depression can begin at any age (the average age is the mid-20s). Without treatment, episodes of depression usually last six months or longer. Following first episodes of depression, many people return to normal and never experience depression again. However, many other people remain depressed. They have recurrent episodes or they become dysthymic (or both). If you are experiencing chronic depression, it is important that you undergo treatment.

Depression May Have a Physical Cause

Before going through therapy for your depression, you should rule out possible physical causes. Your depression may be due to a substance you are abusing (e.g., alcohol, cocaine), or to a prescribed medication (e.g., steroids, tranquilizers). Some medical treatments can trigger depression, as can some medical problems (e.g., thyroid problems, stroke), and some toxins in the environment.

When there is a direct physical cause for your depression, there may be a direct physical cure—stopping the drug abuse, consulting your doctor about possible changes in your medication, correcting the medical condition, removing the toxin. Your should explore all these avenues carefully before relying on therapy.

We recommend that you have a thorough physical examination before beginning therapy for depression. We also recommend that you tell your physician that you are entering therapy and list the symptoms for which you are seeking treatment.

Other Problems That Sometimes Occur with Depression

There are a number of symptoms that tend to occur with depression. You may feel irritable or anxious. You may have stress-related physical problems such as stomachaches or head-aches. You may have an additional problem such as substance abuse, an eating disorder, or an attention deficit disorder. Some depressed people also go through episodes of mania, in which they feel speeded up. Women often become more de-pressed on the days before menstruation. Be sure to inform your therapist if you have any of these problems.

Cognitive-Behavioral Therapy for Depression

Research has shown that cognitive-behavioral therapy is as good or better than other treatments, including antidepressant medication. Cognitive-behavioral therapy is particularly effec-tive in the long run because it provides you with tools that you carry forward from treatment and continue to use. With medi-cation alone, there is a higher risk of relapsing once the medi-cation is discontinued.

Accessing Information about Depression on the Internet.

If you have a computer and access to the Internet, you can get a lot of information about depression. To access an index of patient information on depression and other emotional prob-lems, visit http:\\members.aol.com\SandersonW\cognitive.

SUGGESTED PLEASURABLE ACTIVITIES

1. Tend the garden.
2. Listen to music.
3. Read a book.
4. Go for a walk in a natural setting, such as the woods or a park.
5. Watch a movie.
6. Help someone.
7. Watch sports.
8. Exercise.
9. Play a board game.
10. Watch children play.
11. Play cards.
12. Ride a bicycle.
13. Go for a run.
14. Visit a friend.
15. Call someone on the phone.
16. Sing a song.
17. Play a musical instrument.
18. Play a computer game.
19. Surf the Internet.
20. Watch the sun rise or set.
21. Draw or paint outdoors.
22. Take photographs.
23. Write a letter to someone you love.
24. Get a massage.
25. Visit a new place.
26. Go to an amusement park.
27. Dance.
28. Go for a car ride.
29. Build a model.
30. Fix something that is broken.

31. Work on your car.
32. Attend a lecture.
33. Go to a museum.
34. Enroll in a class.
35. Learn a new craft.
36. Walk on the beach.
37. Solve a brainteaser.
38. Make a videotape.
39. Go to the library.
40. Go to a café.
41. Prepare a healthy meal.
42. Meditate.
43. Listen to a relaxation tape.
44. Go hiking.
45. Go fishing.
46. Go swimming.
47. Attend a political rally.
48. Pray.
49. Have a pleasant daydream.
50. Make love.
51. Take a bath.
52. Contemplate your career path.
53. Start a collection (of books, coins, dolls, etc.).
54. Go shopping for new clothes.
55. Go to a comedy club.
56. Go camping.
57. Arrange flowers.
58. Chop wood.
59. Go to a concert.
60. Redecorate a part of your home.
61. Follow the financial markets.
62. Educate yourself in some aspect of your profession.
63. Go to the racetrack.

64. Go to a casino.
65. Go to a nightclub.
66. Write a poem.
67. Play with an animal.
68. Go to a party.
69. Go scuba diving.
70. Do volunteer work.
71. Go bowling.
72. Go to the theater.
73. Get dressed up.
74. Play chess.
75. Go skating.
76. Go sailing.
77. Plan a trip.
78. Join a club.
79. Play a musical instrument.
80. Go sightseeing.
81. Go to the beauty parlor.
82. Join a discussion group.
83. Go out to a restaurant to eat.
84. Have a sexual fantasy.
85. Write in your journal.
86. Go on a picnic.
87. Do a crossword puzzle.
88. Read the Bible.
89. Go to a religious service.
90. Go horseback riding.
91. Put together a jigsaw puzzle.
92. Study your schoolwork.
93. Birdwatch.
94. Make a fire in the fireplace.
95. Repair something.
96. Participate in a discussion.

97. Read the newspaper.
98. Do an activity with children.
99. Play a game of pool.
100. Perform a community service.
101. Look at the night sky.
102. Go out for ice cream.
103. Have a glass of fine wine (if you do not have a drinking problem).
104. Figure out how something works.
105. Go skiing.
106. Go look at new cars.
107. Go to a country inn.
108. Go rock climbing.
109. Play golf.
110. Go boating.
111. Walk around the city.
112. Go to the zoo.
113. Go to the aquarium.
114. Go to a mall.
115. Invite a friend to visit.
116. Go to the mountains.
117. Tell a joke.
118. Do yardwork.
119. Play a word game.
120. Play frisbee.
121. Tell a story to a child.
122. Compliment someone.
123. Sew.
124. Attend an auction.
125. Give to charity.
126. Do woodworking.
127. Watch television.
128. Listen to talk radio.

129. Look at the stars through a telescope.
130. Have your fortune told.
131. Brush your hair.
132. Join a political group.
133. Go to a twelve-step meeting.
134. Go out on a date.
135. Practice yoga.
136. Go to a martial arts class.
137. Rake the leaves.
138. Go to a bookstore.
139. Go window shopping.
140. Finish some task you have been putting off.
141. Fly an airplane.
142. Observe animals in the wild.
143. Go to the ballet.
144. Fly a kite.
145. Have a conversation.
146. Learn a new song.
147. Build a bonfire at night.
148. Sit on the porch and watch the world.
149. Organize something (your closet, books, music, tools, etc.).
150. Send someone a fax or e-mail.
151. Go to sleep on clean sheets.
152. Manage your finances.
153. Invent a healthful drink.
154. Visit a planetarium.
155. Play tennis.
156. Play a lawn game (croquet, badminton).
157. Experience your five senses, one by one.
158. Dress up in a disguise.
159. Smile.
160. Light a candle and watch the flame.

161. Prepare a lovely table for a meal.
162. Look at beautiful pictures in a book.
163. Hug someone.
164. Make tea or hot chocolate.
165. Sit in the lobby of a beautiful old hotel.
166. Listen to the rain.
167. Walk in the rain, stepping in puddles.
168. Skip.
169. Go on the swings.
170. Eat something sweet.
171. Take a sauna.
172. Buy or make someone a present.
173. Throw a party.
174. Prepare an elaborate holiday celebration.
175. Buy or make yourself a present.
176. Get a pet.
177. Go for a long walk with your dog.
178. Learn how to work an electronic device (cellular phone, VCR, computer, answering machine, etc.).
179. Install a new computer program.
180. Read interesting entries in the encyclopedia.
181. Refinish a piece of furniture.
182. Play baseball.
183. Have a barbecue.
184. Act.
185. Play football.
186. Put lotion on your body.
187. Take a shower.
188. Go to a video arcade.
189. Bake.
190. Play volleyball.
191. Get a good night's sleep.
192. Stay up all night watching movies.

193. Carry out an assertiveness exercise.
194. Go for a train ride along a scenic route.
195. Visit a relative.
196. Talk politics.
197. Conduct an experiment.
198. Play soccer.
199. Practice listening well to another person.
200. Make someone laugh.

PLEASURABLE ACTIVITIES
SELF-MONITORING FORM

Date: _____

Time: _____

Activity: _____

_____

Intensity of Emotion
Ratings

0	25	50	75	100
/_____/_____/_____/_____/				
None	Mild	Moderate	Intense	Very Intense

	Before		After	
	Feeling	Rating	Feeling	Rating
Feelings:	_____	_____	_____	_____
	_____	_____	_____	_____
	_____	_____	_____	_____
	_____	_____	_____	_____

Sense of Mastery: _____

Sense of Pleasure: _____

THOUGHT RECORD

Upsetting Situation	Emotions	Automatic thoughts	Rational Response	Rerate Emotions
(Can be a situation, memory, daydream, or anticipating an event.)	(Rate degree of each emotion from 0 to 100.)			(Rate from 0 to 100).

COMMON COGNITIVE DISTORTIONS
OF DEPRESSION

1. Black or White Thinking: seeing things as either black or white, rather than in shades of gray.

Examples of black or white thinking when depressed: Feeling that if you are not perfect, then you are a complete failure; believing that if you do not have total control over a situation, then you are helpless; feeling that your relationships are either "all good" or "all bad."

2. Overgeneralizing: erroneously assuming that the specifics of one case are true of other cases.

Examples of overgeneralizing when depressed: Because you perform poorly in one situation, you erroneously view yourself as incompetent in other situations. Because a partner rejects you, you feel that no one will ever love you. Because your parent was critical of you, you feel that all authority figures are critical of you. Because something bad happened in one situation, you decide that all similar situations are hopeless.

3. Focusing on the Negative: focusing on the negative aspects of a situation and ignoring the positive aspects, so that you see the situation as more negative than it is realistically.

Examples of focusing on the negative when depressed: You focus only on the bad aspects of yourself, the world, or the people around you, ignoring the good aspects. You focus only on the ways you lack control in a situation, rather than the ways you could (and should) exert control. You focus on the ways you failed to cope with a challenge, rather than acknowledging the ways you succeeded in coping.

4. Jumping to Conclusions: jumping to a conclusion without enough evidence to do so, when other conclusions are also possible.

Examples of jumping to conclusions when depressed: You notice a physical symptom and assume that you have a serious illness. You hear a noise in the house and assume that a criminal has broken in. A friend breaks a date and you assume the person no longer wants to be your friend. Your girlfriend is late coming home and you assume she has gotten into a car accident.

5. Catastrophizing: thinking "what if" bad things happen— usually in great length and imaginative detail.

Examples of catastrophizing: You vividly imagine something bad happening. You experience a manageable event as catastrophic. You imagine the worst possible outcome and then you play it out again and again in your mind.

THE STEPS TO CONSTRUCTING
A RATIONAL RESPONSE

Automatic thoughts: _____

_____

Rate belief in automatic thoughts (0 to 100): _____

What evidence do you have to support your automatic thoughts?

What evidence do you have against your automatic thoughts?

What are some alternative explanations?

Have you made any cognitive distortions?

Can you design a test of your automatic thoughts?

Have you identified a realistic problem? If so, go through the steps of the problem-solving exercise, and write the results here. What solution have you chosen? What steps can you take to carry out this solution?

Has one of your schemas been triggered? Which one? What do you need to do to battle the schema in this case?

Summarized rational response: _____

_____

Rerate belief in automatic thoughts (0 to 100): _____

EARLY MALADAPTIVE SCHEMAS

Disconnection and Rejection

(Expectation that one's needs for security, safety, stability, nurturance, empathy, sharing of feelings, acceptance, and respect will not be met in a predictable manner. Typical family origin is detached, cold, rejecting, withholding, lonely, explosive, unpredictable, or abusive.)

1. Abandonment/Instability (AB)

   The perceived instability or unreliability of those available for support and connection.

   Involves the sense that significant others will not be able to continue providing emotional support, connection, strength, or practical protection because they are emotionally unstable and unpredictable (e.g., angry outbursts), unreliable, or erratically present; because they will die imminently; or because they will abandon the patient in favor of someone better.

2. Mistrust/Abuse (MA)

   The expectation that others will hurt, abuse, humiliate, cheat, lie, manipulate, or take advantage. Usually involves the perception that the harm is intentional or the result of unjustified and extreme negligence. May include the sense that one always ends up being cheated relative to others or "getting the short end of the stick."

3. Emotional Deprivation (ED)

   Expectation that one's desire for a normal degree of emotional support will not be adequately met by others. The three major forms of deprivation are:

   A. *Deprivation of nurturance:* Absence of attention, affection, warmth, or companionship.

B. *Deprivation of empathy:* Absence of understanding, listening, self-disclosure, or mutual sharing of feelings from others.

C. *Deprivation of protection:* Absence of strength, direction, or guidance from others.

4. Defectiveness/Shame (DS)

The feeling that one is defective, bad, unwanted, inferior, or invalid in important respects; or that one would be unlovable to significant others if exposed. May involve hypersensitivity to criticism, rejection, and blame; self-consciousness, comparisons, and insecurity around others; or a sense of shame regarding one's perceived flaws. These flaws may be private (e.g., selfishness, angry impulses, unacceptable sexual desires) or public (e.g., undesirable physical appearance, social awkwardness).

5. Social Isolation/Alienation (SI)

The feeling that one is isolated from the rest of the world, different from other people, and/or not part of any group or community.

Impairied Autonomy and Performance

(*Expectations about oneself and the environment that interfere with one's perceived ability to separate, survive, function independently, or perform successfully. Typical family origin is enmeshed, undermining of child's confidence, overprotective, or failing to reinforce child for performing competently outside the family.*)

6. Dependence/Incompetence (DI)

Belief that one is unable to handle one's everyday responsibilities in a competent manner, without considerable help from others (e.g., take care of oneself, solve daily problems, exercise good judgment, tackle new tasks, make good decisions). Often presents as helplessness.

7. Vulnerability to Harm or Illness (random events) (VH)

Exaggerated fear that "random" catastrophe could strike at any time and that one will be unable to prevent it. Fears focus on one or more of the following: (A) medical (e.g., heart attack, AIDS); (B) emotional (e.g., go crazy); (C) Natural/phobic (elevators, crime, airplanes, earthquakes).

8. Enmeshment/Undeveloped Self (EM)

Excessive emotional involvement and closeness with one or more significant others (often parents), at the expense of full individuation or normal social development. Often involves the belief that at least one of the enmeshed individuals cannot survive or be happy without the constant support of the other. May also include feelings of being smothered by, or fused with, others, or insufficient individual identity. Often experienced as a feeling of emptiness and floundering, having no direction, or in extreme cases questioning one's existence.

9. Failure (FA)

The belief that one has failed, will inevitably fail, or is fundamentally inadequate relative to one's peers, in areas of achievement (school, career, sports, etc.). Often involves beliefs that one is stupid, inept, untalented, ignorant, lower in status, less successful than others.

Impaired Limits

(*Deficiency in internal limits, responsibility to others, or long-term goal orientation. Leads to difficulty respecting the rights of others, cooperating with others, making commitments, or setting and meeting realistic personal goals. Typical family origin is characterized by permissiveness, overindulgence, lack of direction, or a sense of superiority—rather than appropriate confrontation, discipline, and limits in relation to taking responsibility, cooperating in a reciprocal manner, and setting goals. In some cases, child may not have been pushed to tolerate normal levels of discomfort, or may not have been given adequate supervision, direction, or guidance.*)

10. Entitlement/Grandiosity (ET)

    The belief that one is superior to other people; entitled to special rights and privileges; or not bound by the rules of reciprocity that guide normal social interaction. Often involves insistence that one should be able to do or have whatever one wants, regardless of what is realistic, what others consider reasonable, or the cost to others; or an exaggerated focus on superiority (e.g., being among the most successful, famous, wealthy)—in order to achieve power or control (not primarily for attention or approval). Sometimes includes excessive competitiveness toward, or domination of, others: asserting one's power, forcing one's point of view, or controlling the behavior of others in line with one's own desires—without empathy or concern for others' needs or feelings.

11. Insufficient Self-control/Self-discipline (IS)

    Pervasive difficulty or refusal to exercise self-control and frustration tolerance to achieve one's personal goals, or to restrain the excessive expression of one's emotions and impulses. In its milder form, patient presents with an exaggerated emphasis on discomfort-avoidance: avoiding pain, conflict, confrontation, responsibility, or overexertion—at the expense of personal fulfillment, commitment, or integrity.

Other-Directedness

(An excessive focus on the desires, feelings, and responses of others, at the expense of one's own needs—in order to gain love and approval, maintain one's sense of connection, or avoid retaliation. Usually involves suppression and lack of awareness regarding one's own anger and natural inclinations. Typical family origin is based on conditional acceptance: children must suppress important aspects of themselves in order to gain love, attention, and approval. In many such families, the parents' emotional needs and desires—or social acceptance and status—are valued more than the unique needs and feelings of each child.)

12. Subjugation (SB)

Excessive surrendering of control to others because one feels coerced, usually to avoid anger, retaliation, or abandonment. The two major forms of subjugation are:

A. *Subjugation of needs:* Suppression of one's preferences, decisions, and desires.

B. *Subjugation of emotions:* Suppression of emotional expression, especially anger.

Usually involves the perception that one's own desires, opinions, and feelings are not valid or important to others. Frequently presents as excessive compliance, combined with hypersensitivity to feeling trapped. Generally leads to a build-up of anger, manifested in maladaptive symptoms (e.g., passive-aggressive be-havior, uncontrolled outbursts of temper, psychoso-matic symptoms, withdrawal of affection, acting out, substance abuse).

13. Self-sacrifice (SS)

Excessive focus on voluntarily meeting the needs of others in daily situations, at the expense of one's own gratification. The most common reasons are to pre-vent causing pain to others; to avoid guilt from feel-ing selfish; or to maintain the connection with others perceived as needy. Often results from an acute sen-sitivity to the pain of others. Sometimes leads to a sense that one's own needs are not being adequately met and to resentment of those who are taken care of. (Overlaps with concept of codependency.)

14. Approval-seeking/Recognition-seeking (AS)

Excessive emphasis on gaining approval, recogni-tion, or attention from other people, or fitting in, at the expense of developing a secure and true sense of self. One's sense of esteem is dependent primarily on the reactions of others rather than on one's own natu-ral inclinations. Sometimes includes an overemphasis on status, appearance, social acceptance, money, or achievement—as means of gaining approval, admira-tion, or attention (not primarily for power or control). Frequently results in major life decisions that are inauthentic or unsatisfying; or in hypersensitivity to rejection.

Overvigilance and Inhibition

(*Excessive emphasis on controlling one's spontaneous feelings, impulses, and choices in order to avoid making mistakes, or on*

*meeting rigid, internalized rules, and expectations about perfor-
mance and ethical behavior—often at the expense of happiness,
self-expression, relaxation, close relationships, or health. Typical
family origin is grim (and sometimes punitive): performance,
duty, perfectionism, following rules, and avoiding mistakes pre-
dominate over pleasure, joy, and relaxation. There is usually an
undercurrent of pessimism and worry—that things could fall
apart if one fails to be vigilant and careful at all times.)*

15. Negativity/Vulnerability to Error (controllable events)
(NV)

A pervasive, lifelong focus on the negative aspects
of life (pain, death, loss, disappointment, conflict,
guilt, resentment, unsolved problems, potential mistakes, betrayal, things that could go wrong, etc.)
while minimizing or neglecting the positive or optimistic aspects, or an exaggerated expectation—in a
wide range of work, financial, or interpersonal situations that are typically viewed as "controllable"—
that things will go seriously wrong, or that aspects
of one's life that seem to be going well will fall apart
at any time. Usually involves an inordinate fear of
making mistakes that might lead to financial col-
lapse, loss, humiliation, being trapped in a bad situation, or loss of control. Because potential negative
outcomes are exaggerated, these patients are frequently characterized by chronic worry, vigilance,
pessimism, complaining, or indecision.

16. Emotional Inhibition/Overcontrol (EI)

The excessive inhibition of spontaneous action, feeling, or communication—usually to create a sense of
security and predictability; or to avoid making mis-

takes, disapproval by others, catastrophe and chaos, or losing control of one's impulses. The most common areas of excessive control involve (a) inhibition of anger and aggression; (b) compulsive order and planning; (c) inhibition of positive impulses (e.g., joy, affection, sexual excitement, play); (d) excessive adherence to routine or ritual; (e) difficulty expressing vulnerability or communicating freely about one's feelings or needs; or (f) excessive emphasis on rationality while disregarding emotional needs. Often the overcontrol is extended to others in the patient's environment.

17. Unrelenting Standards/Hypercriticalness (US)

The underlying belief that one must strive to meet very high internalized standards of behavior and performance, usually to avoid criticism. Typically results in feelings of pressure or difficulty slowing down; and in hypercriticalness toward oneself and others. Must involve significant impairment in pleasure, relaxation, health, self-esteem, sense of accomplishment, or satisfying relationships.

Unrelenting standards typically present as (a) perfectionism, inordinate attention to detail, or an underestimate of how good one's own performance is relative to the norm; (b) rigid rules and "shoulds" in many areas of life, including unrealistically high moral, ethical, cultural, or religious precepts; or (c) preoccupation with time and efficiency, so that more can be accomplished.

18. Punitiveness (PU)

The belief that people should be harshly punished for making mistakes. Involves the tendency to be angry, intolerant, punitive, and impatient with those people (including oneself) who do not meet one's expectations or standards. Usually includes difficulty forgiving mistakes in oneself or others, because of a reluctance to consider extenuating circumstances, allow for human imperfection, or empathize with feelings.

THE PRINCIPLES OF ASSERTIVENESS

1. *Respect yourself and the other person equally.* This is your overarching goal. When you evaluate how you did afterward, these are the questions to ask yourself: Did I maintain my self-respect? Did I respect the other person?

Here are some criteria you can use to evaluate your performance.

Respecting Yourself: Becoming Less Passive— The "Do's" of Assertiveness

If you truly want to:

1. Express your feelings.
2. Ask for what you need.
3. State your preferences.
4. Assert your rights.

Respecting the Other Person: Becoming Less Aggressive—The "Don'ts" of Assertiveness

1. Do not yell.
2. Do not hit or otherwise physically dominate or intimidate the person.
3. Do not call the person names or otherwise use words to attack him personally.
4. Do not say things simply to hurt the person.
5. Do not lose control of your anger.

2. *Define your goal.* Before you carry out an assertiveness exercise, think it through. What are you trying to accomplish? Be clear within yourself about your goals.

3. *Choose an appropriate setting.* If possible, choose a time and place that gives you privacy, quiet, peace—whatever setting will most help you achieve your assertiveness goals.

4. *If possible, pick a time when the other person is calm.* Try your best to pick a time when the other person is maximally receptive to what you have to say.

5. *Stay calm.* Do not lose control of your anger. If you feel you are going to lose control, leave the situation until you can handle it calmly.

6. *Use assertive body language.* Stand or sit up straight, look the other person in the eye, and speak in a clear and audible voice.

7. *Be as brief and as clear as possible.* The more brief and clear you are, the more powerful your message will be.

8. *Talk about your personal feelings, not about objective "rightness."* Don't preach to the other person about right and wrong. Rather, speak in a personal way. Use "I feel" statements. Say things like: "I feel angry that you . . . I feel uncomfortable when you . . . I don't like it when you . . ."

9. *Do not get defensive.* Do not overjustify your feelings. Do not start listing all the reasons that explain why you are speaking. Your feelings are enough justification. You do not need to speak of any others.

10. *Request specific behavior change.* Tell the person exactly what you want him to do to correct the situation. Be specific and concrete. Criticize the behavior, not the person. Say: "I don't like it when you throw your clothes on the floor"; not, "You are a slob." Say, "Please start putting them in the hamper or putting them away"; not, "Stop being such a slob."

11. *When you want to say something negative, start and end with positives.* This is the "sandwich technique," so called because you sandwich a negative between two positives. Don't make up the positives: use positives that are true.

12. *If the other person protests, simply keep restating your position.* This principle helps you stay on track and stay true to your goal. Don't get lost in arguments the other person raises. Don't go off on tangents. Don't retreat because you have trouble tolerating the other person's anger. No matter what the other person says, just calmly and succinctly keep repeating your point.

SELF-MONITORING FOR ASSERTIVENESS

What is the situation?

What are your feelings about the situation? Rate the intensity of each feeling on a 0 to 100 scale.

What are your automatic thoughts?

Is your thinking in line with the evidence? What are some alternative explanations? Are there errors in your thinking? Write a rational response to your automatic thoughts.

What has your behavior been until now? What are the consequences of behaving this way?

What are your goals? Remember that your main goal is always to behave well—to respect yourself and the other person.

What is the assertive way to meet your goals?

(after completing the assertiveness exercise) How did you do? Did you meet your goals? Did you fulfill the twelve principles of assertiveness?

EDUCATION ABOUT STRESS SYMPTOMS

Stress symptoms are *physical* problems affected by *psychological* stress. Some examples include asthma, headaches, insomnia, irritable bowel and other gastrointestinal problems, panic attacks, anxiety, weight problems, skin problems, chronic pain, high blood pressure, and fatigue. The amount of stress in your life and how you manage that stress psychologically have a significant impact on whether the symptoms ever appear in the first place, and, once they appear, how severe they become.

Stressful events can be positive or negative. Getting married, giving birth to a child, graduating from school, starting a job, buying a house—all these are positive events, and all tend to increase the severity of stress symptoms. Certainly negative life events, such as the breakup of a relationship, the illness or death of someone you love, losing your job, failing in business, falling into debt, also increase the severity of stress disorders.

Stress attacks your body where it is most vulnerable. We are all born with certain physical vulnerabilities. Some of us have slow metabolisms and tend to overeat and become overweight in times of stress. Others have sensitive digestive systems and tend to develop ulcers or irritable bowel. Others have fair, delicate skin, and in times of stress break out in rashes or develop eczema. Stress searches out our natural physical vulnerabilities and capitalizes on them.

We can also develop certain physical vulnerabilities over time, through unhealthy habits or exposure to unhealthy environments. Unhealthy habits include smoking, drinking too much alcohol, having unprotected sex, eating too much junk food, getting too little fresh air or too little exercise. Examples of unhealthy environmental factors include noise, pollution, overcrowding, and crime.

Research shows that relaxation techniques can be helpful in treating stress symptoms. Relaxation techniques include meditation, relaxation training, imagery exercises, hypnosis, biofeedback, and breathing techniques. Research indicates that what is most helpful about these methods is the focusing of attention that is the common ingredient of all of them. Focusing in this way is healing to the body. Practicing these techniques has been shown to decrease stress disorders significantly.

EDUCATION ABOUT PANIC ATTACKS

It is hard to explain to someone who does not have panic attacks what it is like to have one. This is why our patients with panic disorder often feel so alone. It is so hard for them to explain to those around them what it feels like to have the attacks—how frightening they are and how avoiding them at all costs can wreak havoc in their personal and work lives.

This is how one patient named Leonard described a panic attack. If you have panic attacks, then you will probably relate to what he says:

> *Leonard:* I was driving on the highway and I drove into a traffic jam. I don't know what it was, but traffic was down to a crawl. At first there were cars just in front of me, but soon there were cars in back of me, too. I broke into a sweat. My heart was pounding. My first panic attack was in a traffic jam on the highway like this.
>
> What if, I started thinking, what if I had a heart attack in this traffic jam, and I couldn't get out to get help, and no one could get to me.
>
> My heart hurt and my chest was tight. I couldn't catch my breath. My arm went numb. I tried to remember the symptoms of a heart attack. My heart was pounding so hard it felt like it was going to jump out of my chest. And it was beating so fast! It couldn't have been good for my heart to be beating so fast. I had to get out of there but traffic was crawling. Each minute seemed like an eternity.
>
> I really thought I was going to die there in that car.

When Leonard has a panic attack, he feels like he is dying. He believes he is dying—he believes he is having a heart attack. Anyone who believes he is dying is going to panic.

This is how we describe panic to someone who has never had attacks, such as the family members of our panic patients. We say, "Imagine suddenly your life falls into danger. Your elevator gets stuck and the building is burning, a mugger pulls a knife on you, your car swerves out of control. That rush of terror—*that* is how it feels to have a panic attack, except with a panic attack, you feel this way and you don't know why. There is no burning building, no mugger with a gun, no car out of control to explain your fear. The symptoms are apparently happening for no reason. The panic comes out of nowhere, out of the blue. You are eating in a restaurant, watching a movie, standing in a line, driving your car, and suddenly the panic is there."

What Is a Panic Attack?

A panic attack is a sudden rush of intense fear—a feeling that something terrible is about to happen—accompanied by at least some of the following symptoms:

difficulty breathing
heart racing or pounding
pain or tightness in your chest
dizziness or light-headedness
trembling
numbness or tingling sensations
feeling of unreality
tightness or choking feeling in your throat
gastrointestinal disturbance
sweating

hot flashes or chills
fear of dying, going crazy, or losing control

Not everyone fears dying during panic attacks as Leonard does. Some people fear going crazy or losing control. They fear that they are having a nervous breakdown, or that they will mentally drift into unreality and never return to a normal state again. They fear that they will fall, scream, run, cry, get sick, pass out. They are afraid that they will lose control and jump from a height or swerve into traffic with their car. Or they fear becoming unable to function. All of these fears are unrealistic.

What you fear during a panic attack depends largely on which symptoms you have and focus on most. Leonard focuses on his heart symptoms and fears he is having a heart attack. Other people focus on the feeling of unreality and fear they are going crazy, or they focus on the dizziness and fear they are passing out, or they focus on the gastrointestinal symptoms and fear they are getting sick, or they focus on the breathing symptoms and fear they are smothering.

Agoraphobia

Panickers often develop phobias of specific places or activities, such as being alone, being in the middle of crowds (at theaters, stores, concerts, etc.), riding forms of transportation (buses, trains, planes, cars, elevators, ski-lifts), tunnels, bridges, heights, restaurants, traffic jams, taking medication (gas at the dentist, anesthesia, prescription medications), going far from home, going out of the reach of medical help, certain kinds of physical exertion (exercise, sex, amusement park rides), various foods, and waiting in line. If you have panic disorder and you have some of these phobias, then you are agoraphobic.

Agoraphobics are not the same as other kinds of phobics. Other phobics fear specific things in the world that they believe are dangerous. They fear animals because animals can bite; they fear airplanes because airplanes can crash; they fear germs because germs can cause sickness. They can simply avoid the thing that they fear and feel relatively safe. But not agoraphobics. The danger agoraphobics fear comes from within—from their own body, their own mind—in the form of these panic symptoms that seem to come out of nowhere and race out of control. When agoraphobics really explore what they are afraid of, it is always the panic attack itself, and not the danger in the situation. For example, agoraphobics do not fear airplanes because airplanes can crash; they fear them because they might have a panic attack in the plane and be trapped there. It is the panic symptoms, not crashing, that they fear. (Of course, a person might be a panicker and a phobic and fear both.) They believe that the symptoms are dangerous. It is the symptoms that convince them that they are about to die, go crazy, or lose control. Ultimately what they fear is the panic itself. They fear the fear.

Agoraphobics avoid going places where they might have a panic attack and be unable to get out or get help. The places they fear most are those that trap them and those that cut them off from help. These are the two main concerns. They need to know that they can get out of a place and they need to know that they can get help if they need it.

Anticipatory Anxiety

When you have to go somewhere you become very anxious. You may worry for days. You think: "What if I have a panic attack there? Will I be trapped? How embarrassing will it be for me to leave? Will I be able to get help? Will I be able to get home? Will I be alone?" This anticipatory anxiety is a feature of panic disorder, and it can be excruciating. Between attacks you live in dread of the next one; and, although you can guess, you can never be sure where or when the next one is going to strike. You might have safe people or safe places that make you feel better, but you cannot reach a feeling of total safety. Learning to manage your anticipatory anxiety is an important part of treatment.

The Fight-or-Flight and Freeze Responses

Other names for panic attacks are the fight-or-flight and freeze responses. For example, suppose a strange man points a gun at you. In the split second it takes you to understand what is happening, your body begins to react. Nature has prepared your body to react to such emergencies in some very helpful ways. You get a rush of adrenaline, which energizes you. Your senses suddenly become sharper. You see better, hear better. You start to hyperventilate. Your body takes in more oxygen, making more available for organs and muscles. Your heart pumps harder and faster, carrying the oxygen throughout your body. Unnecessary systems such as digestion shut down, preserving all your energy for the emergency at hand.

This fight-or-flight response could save your life in this situation. If you were to run, you could run faster than normal. If you were to fight, you would be stronger and could fight better than usual. Your body would perform at its peak.

Let's suppose that you decide to run. As you turn you see another robber behind you, looking right at you, holding a gun. You are trapped. Nature has prepared you for this situation, too, with another response—the freeze response. It is the opposite of fight-or-flight. Everything in your body slows down. You stop moving (probably a good idea when someone is pointing a gun at you), and may even feel frozen. Things seem unreal, dreamlike (probably a blessing when reality is so bad). Your blood pressure drops (which makes you somewhat dizzy, but would help if you were shot because you would bleed less).

If you have panic disorder, the fight-or-flight or freeze response is what is happening to your body when you have a panic attack.

The Three Laws of Anxiety

These are the three laws of anxiety:

1. Panic is not dangerous.
2. Panic always ends.
3. Exposure decreases anxiety and avoidance increases anxiety.

Panic attacks are not dangerous. The fight-or-flight and freeze responses do not hurt you in any way. In all the vast literature on panic, there is not a single reported case of someone dying, going crazy, or losing control during an attack. Afterward perhaps you are tired, but you have not been harmed.

The panic always passes. Time alone ends a panic attack. The panic always comes to an end, and you always return to your normal state. In fact, panic attacks are by their nature very quick. On their own they end in minutes. If they last longer, you are doing something to maintain them. What you are doing to maintain them has to do with the way you are thinking about the attacks, you are interpreting them as far more dangerous than they really are.

Catastrophic thinking drives your panic attacks. Catastrophizing is jumping to the worst possible conclusion, without the evidence to warrant such a jump. The nickname for catastrophizing is "what if-ing": "What if I am having a heart attack?" "What if the panic never ends?" "What if I am having a nervous breakdown?" "What if I lose control and jump from this height?" "What if I smother to death?" "What if I fall and horribly embarrass myself?" As long as you continue to think catastrophically, you pour fuel on the fire of your panic attacks. Your catastrophic thoughts increase your physical symptoms, which in turn increase your catastrophic thoughts, in a vicious circle that can keep panic going for hours.

Instead, think more realistically. Stop thinking that you are that one special person who will really die, go crazy, or lose control during a panic. Every panicker feels this way. Instead of telling yourself lies that scare you, tell yourself the truth. We recommend that you fill out a thought record every time you experience a panic attack, even a mild one, paying special attention to identifying catastrophic thoughts, and decatastrophizing in the Rational Response column.

Exposure to the symptoms and situations that you fear decreases panic, and avoidance of the symptoms and situations maintains panic. In fact, it is roughly true that, however anxious you are when you leave a situation, that's about how anxious you will be the next time you enter the situation. For example, say you have a fear of going to the mall. You go to the mall, have a major panic attack, and flee at the height of anxiety—say, when you reach an 80 on a 0 to 100 anxiety scale. The next time you go to the mall your anxiety will be about 80, the same level as when you left the mall before.

Now imagine that instead of leaving when you have the panic attack, you stay at the mall. Even if you do nothing to control your anxiety, eventually it will come down, because time alone ends a panic attack. If you stayed at the mall until your anxiety came down, say below 20 on a 0 to 100 anxiety scale, then the next time you went to the mall your anxiety would be about a 20. Whatever level you are at when you leave the situation, that is about the level you will be at the next time you enter it. (The exception is if you let a lot of time pass before entering the situation again. If you go back to avoiding the mall, over time the anxiety will creep back up.)

You Can Master Your Panic

We always tell our panic disorder patients that it is not the panic we are going to treat, but rather their reaction to the panic. They are going to learn to master the panic. The key to mastering panic attacks is to stop running away from them and start facing them and learning to control them. That this can be done we have witnessed hundreds of times. In your treatment you will learn how to master your panic attacks.

MANAGING WORRY

We define worry as a chain of negative thoughts related to fears about the future. Typically you worry that something terrible might happen (you might lose your job), or that something you want might not happen (you might not get a raise).

Worrying can be productive when it motivates you to solve problems and prepare for the future. For example, a productive way to handle worrying about an exam is by studying. If worrying motivates you to study, then it is a good thing. But worry becomes a problem when it is unproductive, or even destructive. Rather than solving problems, chronic worriers often just generate more and more worries.

Since worrying is often accompanied by a mixture of negative emotions (such as fear and dread), and physical sensations (such as muscle tension, pounding heart, and upset stomach), it can have a large impact on how you feel both emotionally and physically. Worrying can have a negative effect on your functioning. It can distract you from your work or rob you of your enjoyment of good things that are happening. Certainly worrying can worsen your depression.

We know from research that, for the most part, people who are worriers do not have more stressful situations in their lives than people who are not worriers. Instead, whether or not you become a worrier seems to be a function of the way you think. Worriers tend to see situations as being more threatening than do nonworriers. In addition, worriers tend to feel they have less control over things that happen in their lives. Finally, worriers typically focus on the most negative aspects of a situation. As a result, they often feel as though a lot of negative things are happening, even though their worry is excessive and unrealistic.

Techniques for Managing Worry

Cognitive techniques

What most people naturally do to deal with worrying is try to distract themselves. However, this only works for a little while, and then you find yourself wrapped up in the worries again. Distracting yourself from your worries doesn't solve them. To overcome your worries, you must confront them.

The best way to deal with your worries is to focus on them and learn to analyze the accuracy of your thinking. Often, the thoughts associated with worry are exaggerated or unrealistic, and you are worrying unnecessarily. If you could become more realistic, you might find that many of your worries are not as serious as you originally thought. Apply what you have learned about cognitive therapy to your thoughts when you are worrying. Filling out Thought Record or The Steps to Constructing a Rational Response forms will help you go through the steps.

Another strategy you can use is decatastrophizing. Worriers catastrophize: they constantly ask themselves, "What if the worst possible thing that can happen does happen?" A manageable problem snowballs into a catastrophe. For example, following a minor argument with her boyfriend, a young woman might start worrying that she and her boyfriend are going to break up, and then she will be alone forever.

Worriers often become stuck in the "what if." They ask themselves what if the worst possible thing happens, and then worry about it endlessly, without ever actually pushing through the what if and asking themselves, "What would actually happen if the worst thing actually happened?" This is called decatastrophizing, or pushing through the what if.

Instead of repetitively worrying, "What if the worst thing happens," or catastrophizing, decatastrophize. This means to ask yourself: "Well, what if the worst thing happens? What would happen then? How would I cope with it?" Having solutions will give you more of a sense of control over the situation, and will help you to feel less helpless.

Behavioral techniques

The main behavioral technique is stimulus control. This means to limit when and where your worrying occurs.

For example, you could decide to set a thirty-minute "worry period," to take place at the same time and at the same place each day. For that thirty-minute period, you would try to spend the entire time worrying. You could close your eyes and think in detail about all the things you are worried about, or you could write out your worries, or you could speak to other people about them. You could do whatever you like to try to fill the entire thirty-minute period with worrying.

But, every time you start to worry at any other time or any other place, you must stop yourself, and instruct yourself to postpone your worrying until your next worry period. If you want to make sure you don't forget the worry, you could write it down. Self-monitoring your worrying will help you learn to identify when you are starting to worry.

To stop worrying during nonworry times, you could distract yourself with more positive activities, such as listening to music or taking a walk outside. Every time the worry comes back, notice it and then distract yourself, until eventually you let the worry go.

APPENDIX II:
SUPPORTING STUDIES:
SELECTED REFERENCES
OF CONTROLLED STUDIES

Beck, A. T., Hollon, S. D., Young, J. E., et al. (1985). Treatment of depression with cognitive therapy and amitriptyline. *Archives of General Psychiatry* 42:142–148.

Blackburn, I. M., Bishop, S., Glen, A. I. M., et al. (1981). The efficacy of cognitive therapy in depression: a treatment trial using cognitive therapy and pharmacotherapy, each alone and in combination. *British Journal of Psychiatry* 139: 181–189.

Dobson, K. S. (1989). A meta-analysis of cognitive therapy for depression. *Journal of Consulting and Clinical Psychology* 46:414–419.

Hollon S. D., DeRubeis, R. J., Evans, M. D., et al. (1992). Cognitive therapy and pharmacotherapy for depression: singly and in combination. *Archives of General Psychiatry* 49:774–781.

REFERENCES

American Psychiatric Association. (1994). *Diagnostic and Statistical Manual of Mental Disorders, Fourth Edition*. Washington, DC: American Psychiatric Association.

Barlow, D. H., and Craske, M. G. (1989). *Mastery of Your Anxiety and Panic*. Albany, NY: Graywind.

Beck, A. T. (1976). *Cognitive Therapy and the Emotional Disorders*. New York: International Universities Press. (Soft-cover: New American Library, Dutton.)

———— (1995). *Cognitive Therapy: Basics and Beyond*. New York: Guilford.

Beck, A. T., Rush, A. J., Shaw, B., and Emery, G. (1979). *Cognitive Therapy of Depression*. New York: Guilford.

Bernstein, D. A., and Borkovec, T. D. (1973). *Progressive Relaxation Training*. Champaign, IL: Research Press.

Burns, D. D. (1980). *Feeling Good*. New York: William Morrow. (Soft-cover: New American Library, Penguin.)

Jacobson, E. (1938). *Progressive Relaxation*. Chicago: University of Chicago Press.

Lewinsohn, P. L., Munoz, R., Youngren, M. A., and Zeiss, A. M. (1992). *Control Your Depression*. New York: Fireside.

Piaget, J. (1967). *Six Psychological Studies*. New York: Random House.

Young, J. E. (1990). *Cognitive Therapy for Personality Disorders: A Schema-Focused Approach*. Sarasota, FL: Professional Resource Exchange.

Young, J. E., Beck, A. T., and Weinberger, A. (1993). Depression. In *Clinical Handbook of Psychological Disorders*, ed. D. H. Barlow, pp. 240–277. New York: Guilford.

Young, J. E., and Klosko, J. S. (1993). *Reinventing Your Life*. New York: New American Library, Dutton.

INDEX

deepening relaxation, 126
healing imagery, 129–131
pleasant imagery, 127–129
progressive muscle
relaxation, 121–126
stress symptom education,
116–118
stylistic concerns, 119–120
Role playing, assertiveness
training exercises,
104–105

Schemas and assumptions,
184–192
autonomy and performance,
impaired, 185–186
cognitive-behavioral treatment, session 6, 71–79
disconnection and rejection,
184–185
limits, impaired, 187–188
other-directedness, 188–189
overvigilance and inhibition,
189–192
Self-control, impaired limits,
schemas and assumptions,
187–188
Self-discipline, procrastination,
137
Self-monitoring and self-
evaluation
assertiveness training,
98–101
pleasurable activities, 179
Self reinforcement, productivity
improvement, 142
Self-sacrifice, other-
directedness, 189

Session timing, cognitive-
behavioral treatment, 24
Skinner, B. F., 3
Somatic self-calming
techniques, anger
management, 112–114
Stimulus control, productivity
improvement, 139
Stressors, general, panic
attacks, 155–156
Stress symptom education
described, 197–198
relaxation techniques, 116–
118
Subjugation, other-
directedness, 188–189
Substance abuse,
contraindication for
treatment, 23
Suicide
assessment and contract, 33–
39
ideation of, depression
symptom, 30, 169
Symptom persistence, dealing
with, 18–19

Tension headache, healing
imagery, 129
Termination, cognitive-
behavioral treatment,
session 8, 87–88
Therapeutic relationship, 6–14
collaborative empiricism, 9–
12
generally, 6–9
guided discovery, 12–14
Thought record, 180

About the Authors

Janet Klosko, Ph.D., received her doctorate from the State University of New York at Albany, where she worked under the mentorship of Dr. David Barlow at the Center for Stress and Anxiety Disorders. She is currently the co-director of the Cognitive Therapy Center of Long Island and senior therapist at the Cognitive Therapy Center of New York. She is the co-author of *Reinventing Your Life*, a self-help book on cognitive-behavioral therapy.

William C. Sanderson, Ph.D., is Associate Professor of Psychology at Rutgers University in New Jersey. Specializing in the treatment of anxiety and depressive disorders, he has published five books and more than sixty chapters and articles. An appointed advisor to the *DSM-IV* Anxiety Disorders Workgroup, Dr. Sanderson is currently a member of the Task Force on Psychological Interventions, APA Division of Clinical Psychology.